ACHIEVING INDIGENOUS STUDENT SUCCESS

A Guide for Secondary Classrooms

Pamela Rose Toulouse

PORTAGE & MAIN PRESS

Portage & Main Press gratefully acknowledges the financial support of the Province of Manitoba through the Department of Sport, Culture and Heritage and the Manitoba Book Publishing Tax Credit, and the Government of Canada through the Canada Book Fund (CBF) for our publishing activities.

Printed and bound in Canada by Friesens
Cover and interior design by Relish New Brand Experience

Library and Archives Canada Cataloguing in Publication

Toulouse, Pamela Rose, author
Achieving indigenous student success : a guide for secondary classrooms / Pamela Rose Toulouse.

ISBN 978-1-55379-656-5 (paperback)

1. Native peoples--Education--Canada. 2. Education, Secondary--Activity programs. 3. Classroom management--Canada. I. Title.

E96.2.T69 2016 371.829'97071 C2015-908778-3

22 21 20 19 2 3 4 5 6

PORTAGE & MAIN PRESS

1-800-667-9373
www.portageandmainpress.com
Winnipeg, Manitoba
Treaty 1 Territory and homeland of the Métis Nation

CONTENTS

ACKNOWLEDGMENTS

I wish to take this opportunity to say, "Chi-Meegwetch" ("Thank You" in Ojibwe) to several individuals and groups for their valuable contributions to this book, *Achieving Indigenous Student Success: A Guide for Secondary Classrooms.*

On the professional front:

At Portage & Main Press, I would like to recognize Annalee Greenberg and Catherine Gerbasi for making this book possible. To Leigh Hambly, also at P & M Press, thank you for being such a wonderful editor and supporter.

To Indigenous leads and teachers in the provinces/territories, your commitment to students and our communities will leave its mark for many years to come.

To non-Indigenous educators who are passionate about learning and not afraid to embrace change that honours all students and fosters respectful spaces.

To Laurentian University, my workplace, for providing me with environment and conditions to research and publish.

On the personal front:

To my students (past, present, future) who have given me the vision and incentive to teach and be myself. You make coming to work a pleasure and an honour.

To those who advocate for the humane treatment of all peoples (this includes our fur families, like mine), your work is truly Creator driven.

To my parents, Nelson Toulouse and Dorothy Toulouse (nee Recollet – in the Spirit World), thank you for teaching me the value of leadership and kindness.

To my partner, Luc Watier, your positive outlook on the world and dedication to our little family makes my heart smile every day.

PREFACE

I have been so fortunate to see monumental changes in education over the past 40 (and then some) years. I think back to my own days in high school, which, for me, were quite painful. I was a teenager from the reserve and so unsure of myself. I was also dealing with a lot of trauma. This was done in isolation, as I really didn't trust most people and had very little self-esteem. Canada's Indigenous peoples, during that time, were very rarely discussed in a positive light (if discussed at all). There was a clear divide between students and their origins (race, class, appearance, geographical locations, other). For me, high school was not the good old days, but the "I-can't-wait-to-get-out-of-here" days.

Today, I see our Indigenous youth struggle with new sets of challenges. I am, however, most impressed by their strength and resiliency. This truly is a new world where equity, diversity, and commitment to social justice are in the forefront. In the past decade, I have borne witness to and been part of a movement that has seen Indigenous world-view infused in classrooms at all levels. I am lucky I work with educators, administrators, and organizations that work diligently at ensuring Indigenous students and communities thrive. I am also honoured to work with children, youth, and young adults who leave me breathless with their compassion, dedication, and humour.

I have been in the field of education for a little over 20 years. I started out as a classroom teacher, worked in administration (at a university and tribal council level), and continued to teach and advise students in various capacities. Most recently, I have had the distinct pleasure of learning with the most wonderful teacher candidates and also of consulting with school boards in the area of Indigenous pedagogy. This evolving role I occupy has given me a new lens to see the progress and challenges our schools have made – and, indeed, still face.

Resources and professional development that are hands-on, teacher friendly, and respectful of Indigenous world-view remain an area for growth. *Achieving Indigenous Student Success: A Guide for Secondary Classrooms* is a much-needed contribution to this type of pedagogical literature and culturally infused material gap. The chapters, lesson plans, and resources offer high-school teachers practical strategies and advice they can implement immediately. This book truly is the culmination of my own personal experiences and professional development, and a reflection of the voices of educators, youth, and other committed stakeholders I have listened to over the years. I have written this text so that "take-aways" – those strategies and ideas that can be applied immediately – are evident and immediate.

In conclusion, I thank you, the reader, for taking this journey with me, and I do hope our youth in secondary schools benefit from your continued dedication.

INTRODUCTION

Who This Book Is For

Every province and territory in Canada has a government agency (department or ministry) committed to education. Each of these departments or ministries has policies, curricula, or positions that focus on Indigenous students and their success in schools. Unfortunately, resources on Indigenous student success, especially at the secondary level, are difficult to find. Such information is urgently needed – especially when the majority of teachers of Indigenous students in Canada are non-Indigenous.

Achieving Indigenous Student Success: A Guide for Secondary Classrooms has been written to help fill this gap in educational resources. This book is for all secondary teachers who have Indigenous students in their classrooms and/or are looking for ways to infuse Indigenous content into their courses. Educators in all settings will find innovative ways to engage their students with the teaching/learning pedagogy presented. Although the primary focus of this book is the needs of Indigenous students, the ideas are best practices that can be applied in classrooms of any makeup.

How to Use This Book

Achieving Indigenous Student Success: A Guide for Secondary Classrooms is divided into two sections. Part 1: Program Foundations, offers culturally relevant pedagogical practices for teachers to implement and also suggests ways to support learners in the classroom. Part 1 covers chapters 1–5, and includes the following topics:

- teaching strategies
- lesson ideas
- contributions of Indigenous peoples
- culturally appropriate mental-health activities
- provincial/territorial best practices
- examples of how to differentiate instruction
- Bloom's Taxonomy with culturally specific questions
- wise practices in the retention/transition/graduation continuum
- Indigenous resources by secondary-course subject
- appropriate themes for curricular connections

Part 2: Culturally Appropriate Secondary Lessons by General Subject, includes a number of lesson plans with suggested grade modifications.

These lesson plans can be implemented/adapted immediately and effectively in the secondary environment. All lessons have the following:

- Indigenous concept, teaching, historical fact, traditional use, present application identified
- the time, space, materials/resources, considerations, cautions listed
- step-by-step plans
- strategies for engagement, inquiry questions, terminology, classroom management recorded
- assessment/evaluation, curricular extensions, and potential adaptations documented

Appendix A includes a map of Turtle Island and 12 regional maps showing the traditional locations of the Indigenous Nations living on Turtle Island. Appendix B consists of two lists: "Indigenous Names for First Nations and Inuit of Canada" and "Alternative Names for Indigenous Peoples of the United States."

PART 1

PROGRAM FOUNDATIONS: CHAPTERS 1 TO 5

INTRODUCTION TO PART 1: PROGRAM FOUNDATIONS

The chapters that follow offer secondary-classroom teachers strategies, theories, ideas, and resources that honour Indigenous world-view. The pedagogy being discussed for implementation in schools is relevant for all learners, especially in educational spaces devoted to inclusion and equity.

Chapter 1. Indigenous Pedagogy and Classroom Considerations provides an overview of

- a holistic way to approach course and lesson planning
- the spiritual aspect of planning that begins with identifying a culturally appropriate resource and learner concepts
- the physical aspect of planning that has the educator determining the time needed, space(s) required, materials needed, and considerations/cautions
- the emotional aspect, also known as the three-step plan, which has the teaching strategies, inquiry questions, key terms, and classroom-management techniques
- the intellectual aspect, which has the assessment for/as/of strategies, curricular extensions, and suggested ways to infuse Indigenous contributions across the subjects

Chapter 2. Indigenous Self-Esteem and Mental Health Activities provides an overview of

- the living concepts of *bimaadziwin* and *windigos* in an adolescent's life
- appropriate secondary strategies in teaching these Indigenous concepts
- national Indigenous mental-health resources and initiatives to implement in secondary classrooms
- a culturally appropriate model and description of the stages in a human being's life
- how to create a living profile and use this as a critical self-esteem and mental-health analysis tool

Chapter 3. Differentiated Instruction and Bloom's Taxonomy provides an overview of

- practical strategies in the content, the process, the product, and the learning environment aspects of differentiated instruction (DI)
- examples of how to implement DI on a continuum with Indigenous resources as the focus, as well as subject-based suggestions

- the six levels of Bloom's Taxonomy and the connections to the Ojibwe living wheel, including examples at each level
- applying Bloom's question stems and respectfully integrating the innovations of the 500 Nations
- partnerships and materials that are culturally appropriate and models emulating a differentiated approach in secondary education

Chapter 4. Attrition, Retention, Transition, and Graduation Continuum provides an overview of

- the factors that lead Indigenous students to exit secondary schools early
- the practices that provide a foundation for Indigenous student success in high schools
- retention strategies that focus on curriculum/pedagogy, extra-curricular support, parental/guardian/community engagement, culturally safe spaces, and career events/cooperative activities
- transition strategies that focus on national examples for changes from elementary to secondary and secondary to postsecondary (or to work)
- graduation strategies that focus on a balanced approach through understanding our locations, deconstructing colonial constructs, and contributing to learner communities

Chapter 5. Indigenous Themes and Material Resources provides an overview of

- select Indigenous texts, resources, and materials for grades 9 through 12 in English, Math, Science, History, Geography, Health and Physical Education, Integrated Arts (Music, Drama, Visual Arts), as well as Professional Development for teachers
- connecting these material resources to Indigenous Lifelong Learning Concepts (First Nations, Métis, and Inuit)

Chapter 1.

INDIGENOUS PEDAGOGY AND CLASSROOM CONSIDERATIONS

An Holistic Approach

What is holism? When Indigenous communities speak of the need for classrooms to take a holistic approach, what do they mean? Just what does a holistic approach look like? Each Nation of the 500 Nations on Turtle Island (North America and part of the Mesoamericas) has its own explanation; however, two commonalties do exist: consideration and respect for the whole person (Whitley 2014).

As an Ojibwe woman, I have been raised with my own world-view, traditions, experiences, and history.

What I bring to this chapter on Indigenous pedagogy is my understanding of *what works* at the secondary level. The model and strategies for classroom consideration are firmly supported by a growing body of literature on holistic and culturally competent learning spaces. This pedagogical approach supports Indigenous student success and is consistent with the research on effective teaching practices in equity-based classrooms (Nardozi et al. 2014).

Many educators feel ill equipped to teach about Indigenous peoples and their contributions to the world. The reasons range from fear of getting it wrong, to lack of resources, to lack of clarity in how to approach Indigenous communities, to uncertainty about connections between Indigenous resources and the provincial/territorial curricula (Dion, Johnston, and Rice 2010). These are legitimate concerns and completely normal for a teacher committed to student achievement and diversity. In fact, the first step to planning an Indigenous approach to any classroom is to identify the barriers (e.g., fears, assumptions, potential blocks) one faces. This is a humbling act in which an individual is forced to confront the unknown/known and the reasons for this discomfort.

Educators often do not see that their current approaches to learning, via effective strategies and dynamic resources, complement Indigenous students and their success in the classroom. Many educators are already implementing pedagogical approaches and teaching tools that support Indigenous students. What needs to grow, however, is a conscious assessment of areas we do well in and areas that require more work. This level of reflection and transformation is the mark of a teacher who is committed to the areas of student achievement and social change (Santoro et al. 2011).

Important Note! **Self-identification includes the term an Indigenous person wishes to be referred to. For the author, Pamela Rose Toulouse, the words *Ojibwe* and *Anishinaabe* are interchangeable. Both are the ways she wants to be identified.**

The Foundation for an Effective Learning Cycle

The Foundation for an Effective Learning Cycle (see figure 1.1) has its foundations rooted in the teachings of the Ojibwe Medicine Wheel. It represents the holistic world-view presented in this book. The Medicine Wheel is a circle that embodies the teachings of equality, interconnectedness, and the cycles of life. It is composed of four quadrants, each representing a cardinal direction of north, south, east, or west. In turn, each direction represents different elements of life, including spirit animals, medicine, life stages, and colours. The Medicine Wheel represents the balance between the spiritual, intellectual, emotional, and physical aspects of ourselves.

The four aspects needed for effective teaching are: spiritual, physical, emotional, and intellectual (see figure 1.1).

Important Note!
"Sacred and alive" refers to the lived application of Indigenous teachings in a person's day-to-day existence. Here, for example, it means the teachings of the Medicine Wheel and living a balanced life with attention to the spiritual, physical, emotional, and intellectual aspects of the self.

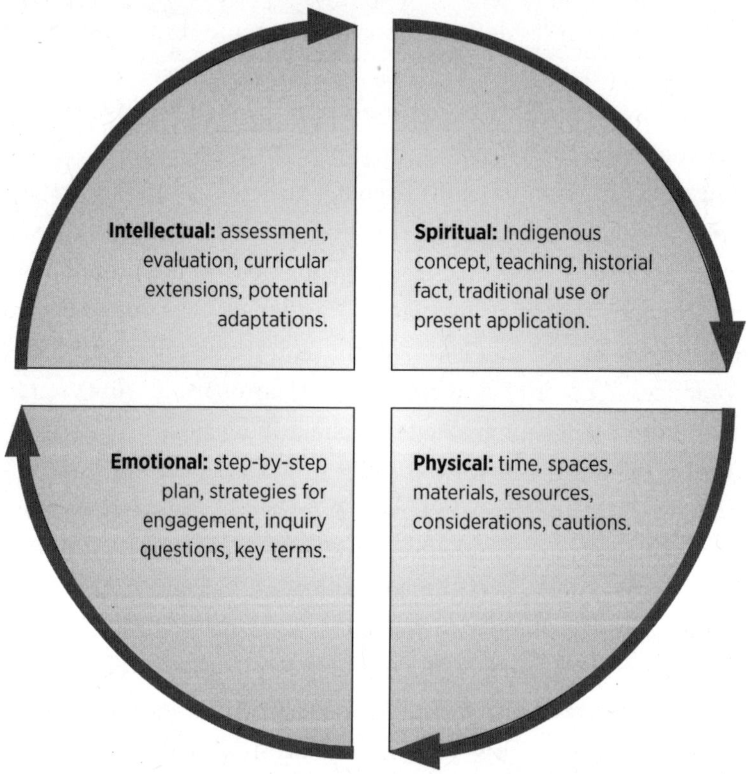

Figure 1.1. *The Foundation for an Effective Learning Cycle. This living model is based upon the teachings of the Ojibwe Medicine Wheel and is the foundation for an effective learning cycle (unit) or lesson plan at the secondary level. A living model refers to a particular Indigenous teaching, tradition, or aspect of world-view that is sacred and alive. It is organic and adapts to growth and time.*

The Spiritual

The spiritual aspect of the Learning Cycle model (see figure 1.1) is where educators need to start when planning units and lessons aimed at infusing

Indigenous world-view into the curriculum (Assembly of First Nations 2012a; Kanu 2011). This typically begins with the selection of a resource (e.g., book, video, website, human, geographical, artifact) or event the educator finds inspiring, interesting, familiar, or is comfortable with. When examining the resource or event, it is critical to identify its key (or multiple key) Indigenous concepts, teachings, historical facts, traditional uses, or present applications. This represents the culturally appropriate learning outcome(s) or goal(s) that will be made explicit with the students. How is this done? What are the steps or methods that can be used to identify these concepts/other in a respectful manner? The following are some suggestions:

- Consult with your Indigenous leads or department or personnel entrusted with Indigenous education to find out the resources available to you. These resources and materials have already been vetted by a stakeholder. Use the resources to help you identify the key concepts, teachings, facts, and/or other, as well as to help you select appropriate teaching strategies.
- Form a relationship with a local Indigenous community, organization, education counsellor, and/or cultural representative, and identify the opportunities that can be explored in a reciprocal partnership with you and your students. Firsthand knowledge and participation by Indigenous peoples offer curricular insights that cannot be duplicated by a material resource.
    - Books: Begin with the summary or abstract at the front/back of the text. Most authors are instrumental in constructing the summary and capture the essence of the resource.
    - Videos (online and real): Read the précis that describes the content, and seek out viewer reviews for feedback on what others have gained from the viewing. Identify key Indigenous insights from these statements that are to be conveyed to your students.
    - Websites and social-media tools: Seek out information on the author or creator of the website/social-media app and the information therein. You want to establish that the content is authentic and comes from a verified Indigenous source. When planning activities with Indigenous websites and/or social media as the platform, isolate the critical teachings you want your students to receive in the exercise. These teachings are in the descriptions of the website and/or social-media apps.
    - Indigenous resource people: Review the resource person's biography and the services he or she offers. From this information, establish a learning goal with your students. First-person participation ensures this learning goal will be far exceeded by students' personal and highly skilled presentations.
    - Geographical resources (real and online): Select the critical facts, uses, or teachings of an Indigenous geographical site. These are often found in the

material (e.g., pamphlets, websites, other publications) associated with the site or as communicated by Indigenous community members. Land-based activities – teaching strategies and culminating tasks that take place in the environment – are critical to establishing Indigenous connections and understandings. These activities also provide opportunities to foster experiential learning.

- Artifacts (real and online): Record the use of the item as it is summarized (e.g., by the museum, website, video), and then cross-reference this information with your Indigenous lead or Indigenous partner. Ensure that introducing this artifact to your class is appropriate. For example, if you choose to have quill boxes as part of your math lesson, ensure the use and teaching of these items are included and verified. If you choose to have a traditional drum as part of your music lesson, check local Indigenous protocols to find out how this drum is to be introduced (if at all or if a substitute can be provided).
- Events (live and virtual): Identify the intent/purpose of the event from the source – organization, site, other (e.g., Why is this event being held?). This becomes the foundation of a flexible learning goal for your students. For example, if you decide to take your students to an Indigenous play or artistic presentation, share the purpose and significance and allow for an elaboration on this experience later. The impacts of these events will clearly outweigh the initially identified purpose(s).

As educators, we often feel the need to be completely knowledgeable about our subjects and are uncomfortable with content we do not have expertise in. The beauty of incorporating Indigenous resources is that the learning experience becomes a co-construction of knowledge and memories between the teacher and learners (Scully 2012). It becomes a place of growing together in a process of discovery. The first time you introduce a resource (with its cultural concept, use, or application) as part of a lesson, it will be enlightening. The second time it is introduced, your own knowledge and understanding will be enhanced, changing the experience in a different but equally meaningful manner. The benefits of infusing Indigenous world-view as part of your courses will result in rich personal connections to the material for both you and your students (Lowan 2010). Taking the risk and the time and building relations are critical to this stage.

The Physical

The physical aspect of the Learning Cycle model (see figure 1.1) is concerned with the time and materials/resources needed, space(s) required, considerations, and cautions. It is a comprehensive inventory of all the tools you will need to carry out this learning cycle (unit) or lesson plan. Here are some questions you need to consider:

- Do I need to book a computer lab?
- Do I need to secure math manipulatives?
- Do students require permission slips to attend an event?
- How much time is required for this lesson?
- Do I need to set up my class in groups, in rows, or in a circle?
- What resources do I need in order for my students to complete the tasks?
- Are there enough materials available for us to complete the lesson?
- Do I require an honorarium for the guest speaker?

In terms of considerations and cautions, these are the wise practices teachers use as part of a culturally competent classroom (St. Denis 2011). These practices are also known as the "issues" – the do's and don'ts of teaching Indigenous content (see figure 1.2). Nationally, many school boards have developed guidelines for their educators that are explicit in how to respectfully engage with Indigenous peoples and their knowledge(s). I am fortunate to live in a province where several of these leading documents have been developed and implemented. Issues range from the impact of Indigenous images in classroom resources (e.g., presence of stereotypes), to teaching strategies that are culturally appropriate (e.g., using a differentiated approach), to using Indigenous terms and language (e.g., self-identity of local Nations), to authenticity of resources (who wrote the material). For each issue, there is always a do and a don't (Rainbow District School Board 2013).

Authenticity

DO

Invite Indigenous Elders, Métis Senators, and resource people into the classroom.

Use Indigenous resources (e.g., books, videos) that include Indigenous voices.

DON'T

Appropriate (make something that is not yours) sacred items such as eagle feathers.

Promote resources that perpetuate stereotypes (e.g., cartoons of Indians smoking a peace pipe).

Images

DO

Discuss the impact of stereotypes and their dehumanizing effect (e.g., sports mascots, advertisements, dollar-store items like dream-catchers).

Include present photos and representations of Indigenous peoples that reflect their diversity.

DON'T

Let stereotypes go unchallenged.

Use stereotypical resources that promote imagery of savages, sexualized Indian women, Manifest Destiny, and *terra nullius*.

Figure 1.2. *Do's and Don'ts. This model represents two of the many issues that may arise when teaching Indigenous content or selecting resources. Being critically literate and informed is key to this approach.*

The Emotional

The emotional aspect of the Learning Cycle model (see figure 1.1) involves the strategies used to engage your students with the content. This is often referred to as a "three-part lesson" (which, in this book, includes the key terms, the inquiry questions, and the step-by-step plan). However, there are always several points for learning opportunities to occur. Here are some of the areas you need to consider when constructing a lesson respectful of Indigenous content (Toulouse 2014):

- What strategies will I use in the lesson?
- How will instruction be differentiated?
- Are assessment practices embedded in the content?
- What terms do I want my students to take away?
- What inquiry questions will become the platform for this lesson to flourish?

When designing a learning cycle (unit) or lesson, the same queries apply and become the focus of effective and meaningful student engagement.

Teaching and learning strategies come from many schools of thought. We have differentiated approaches, multiple intelligences, Bloom's Taxonomy, and so many more. However, my own research and practice have evolved into a culturally constructed one, where dynamic strategies that focus on community building are the foundation (Alberta Education 2011). My learning cycles (units) and lesson plans are consistent in that they are explicit with the approaches to engagement, the questioning, the terms, the identification of mini-lessons, the scaffolding of knowledge, and the inclusion of classroom management as critical to student success with Indigenous resources/world-view.

Learning cycles (units) embedded with Indigenous content provide amazing opportunities to engage and immerse students in meaningful ways. Lesson plans that are carefully created and infused with Indigenous resources can also provide opportunities to explore Indigenous concepts in an authentic manner. The longer and more in-depth students interact with and explore Indigenous world-view and resources (and are able to make personal connections), the more impact Indigenous world-view and resources have on students (Kanu 2011). This commitment to infusing Indigenous perspectives provides the space for conscientious learning to take place; that is, action based with social-justice awareness.

For every lesson, it is ideal to identify two to four key terms essential to student learning (e.g., self-determination, treaties, sovereignty). Also, two to four key questions (points for inquiry) are critical to record, as they provide opportunities for further understanding of the content (i.e., ranging from knowledge, to application, to evaluation). The terms and questions will vary with the resource content but are significant in framing the lesson focus. In terms of teaching/learning strategies, it is optimal to have mini-lessons (as facilitated by the teacher, and that in some instances may be called "direct instruction") with a range of student-centred activities that are dynamic, reflective, interactive, hands-on, and build relationships between learners (Whitley 2014). Some examples (with pedagogical advice) of this approach are included in figure 1.3.

Learning Styles	• Develop a classroom profile of the preferred learning styles and potential resources you can draw upon. • Develop a list of teaching strategies that complement Indigenous learners and ESL/ELL, special-needs, and at-risk students.
Cooperative Strategies	• Identify the current resources on cooperative learning you have on hand. Some examples of these strategies are: jigsaw, literature circles, round robin, think/pair/share, numbered heads, buddy system.
Thinking Skills	• Compile a list of the critical-thinking and inquiry/research resources available to you. Some examples of these are: brainstorming, visual organizers, think alouds, concept mapping, graphing, mind maps, problem solving.
Integrated Arts	• Create an inventory of arts- and activity-based materials (including PD packages) you can use. Some examples of these resources/strategies are: tableaux, field trips, sketching to learn, activity centres, collages, debates, role-playing, games, reader's theatre, simulations, mask making.
Independent Learning	• List the ways and methods you have students do independent work. Some examples of these strategies are: journals, portfolios, homework, silent reading, note making, reports, learning logs, memorization.

Figure 1.3. *Interactive Teaching Strategies. The diagram above provides a starting point for educators to consider when selecting a range of activities to facilitate an Indigenous-focused lesson and/or learning cycle. (Adapted from Ontario Ministry of Education 2002).*

Mini-lessons are critical to the delivery of content and are facilitated by the teacher. They are the direct instructional opportunities of the teacher and can range from 8 to 20 minutes. Mini-lessons provide opportunities to scaffold the knowledge (e.g., key learning goals, concepts, facts) into the lesson (Santoro et al. 2011). Each mini-lesson is accompanied or followed by a student-centred activity (see figure 1.3). Some examples of teacher-directed strategies are:

- use of technology-aided presentations (e.g., PPT, Prezi, video, radio, social media, software applications, multimedia)
- lectures
- demonstrations
- advance organizers
- guided reading, writing, exploration
- practices/drills
- storytelling
- textbooks
- worksheets
- read alongs/alouds
- reviews
- tutorials
- guest speakers
- book talks
- flash cards
- visualizations

The above list is not all encompassing. However, it is a good starting point for reflecting on and assessing the direct-instruction tools you use and/or need to change.

Classroom management also requires explicit instructions in this section of the plan (whether it is a learning cycle or lesson). Classroom management refers to how you organize the lesson and ranges from movement of paper, to structuring of groups, to how students can get your attention, to logical rewards and/or consequences for behaviour (Alberta Education 2011). It is your go-to plan and also highlights the transitions that make the lesson run smoothly. For example, when you want students to focus on you, what strategies do you use? Do you play a sound bite that means it is your time for presenting? Do you play a short video clip? Do you have students repeat back a phrase? The transition should involve something fun and, ideally, informative that relates to the lesson content. Getting student attention quickly and focusing on the next task maximizes your time in class. It also gives you the space to make instructions clear, check for understanding, and highlight the value of that learning time.

The Intellectual

The intellectual aspect of the Learning Cycle model (see figure 1.1) refers to the assessment/evaluation considerations and curricular extensions/adaptations of the learning cycle (unit) or lesson plan. Assessment and learning go hand in hand (Assembly of First Nations 2012a). They are embedded in and focus on student achievement. The three levels of assessment/evaluation are *assessment for learning, assessment as learning,* and *assessment of learning.* Assessment for learning typically occurs before the lesson (or learning cycle) or during the introduction section of a lesson. This allows the teacher to identify students' prior knowledge and get to know where the students are at in terms of the new content. Assessment as learning typically occurs during the lesson. It includes self-assessment, peer assessment, and other strategies students engage in to check their learning during the lesson (or unit). Assessment of learning typically occurs at the end of the lesson (or unit). It is the analysis of students achieving the curricular expectations. At every level in the lesson (or unit), students are directly involved in the evaluation of their own learning. This co-constructed process is facilitated by the teacher, and the student's growth and achievements are always the focus (Nardozi et al. 2014).

In terms of curricular extensions and potential adaptations, there are distinctions. Curricular extensions refer to ways the Indigenous content/resources can be adjusted for other subject areas, or ways additional activities can be developed in that same subject area. Grade adaptations refer to the ways the lesson can change to suit various grades and levels (e.g., Is your course open? Is it workplace-focused? Is it a university-level course at your high school?). These adaptations are integral to ensuring the Indigenous content/resource is transferable to other secondary-classroom settings.

Every subject and course has its own type of assessment for/as/of learning practices. Science may use a learning log as the main tool. History may use the KWL chart as a primary resource. English may use the portfolio. Health and Physical Education may use the performance task. However, most will have learning goals, success criteria, achievement charts, and exemplars in common. Although subject-specific assessment and evaluation tools are important to draw upon, a differentiated approach to assessment crosses those disciplines and offers student selected alternatives as well (Scully 2012). Some other examples of assessment for/as/of learning strategies/tools to consider are:

- conferencing
- developmental continua
- inventories and surveys
- demonstrations and performances
- question and answer
- graphic organizers
- oral presentations
- cloze procedures
- quizzes
- checklists and records
- retells
- journals (written, pictorial, sound)
- photo montages or collages
- response cards
- entry/exits slips
- bodily-kinesthetic (e.g., thumbs up, thumbs down, stamp feet, clap hands)

Important Note!
Ontario's Ministry of Education document called *Growing Success: Assessment, Evaluation and Reporting in Ontario's Schools* (First Edition Covering Grades 1 to 12) and online learning videos are valuable tools to refer to regarding ways to differentiate assessment.

- flip books
- turn n' talk
- quick writes
- dry-erase boards or clipboards for recording responses
- simulation/games
- critical incidents/case studies

These are only a few examples of ways to differentiate assessment. Teachers who adopt an inclusive approach know student achievement and the provision of diversity in practices are key to learner success (St. Denis 2011).

Indigenous Innovations Across the Curriculum

We began this chapter with an elaboration on the successful factors that contribute to learning cycles (units) and lessons that infuse Indigenous content. This discussion is framed within the spiritual, physical, emotional, and intellectual domains. The research further suggests Indigenous pedagogy is firmly rooted in honouring the local Indigenous populations (i.e., First Nations, Métis, Inuit) and by incorporating a variety of authentic resources (both material and nonmaterial). However, this pedagogical model should also incorporate an understanding or appreciation of the contributions of the 500 Nations on Turtle Island (Toulouse 2014). The land on which we all co-exist and many of its place names and innovations are the result of Indigenous traditional knowledge. Most secondary-school courses are devoid of this content. However, I believe Indigenous innovations need to be explored and discussed in the context of their contemporary applications (see figure 1.4). Building relationships and truths between students of all backgrounds depends upon this content (Lowan 2010).

The contributions that come from Indigenous peoples in Canada are immense. It is important that educators begin with local contributions, then widen the discussion to incorporate wider-ranging examples. (Secondary resources like Keoke and Porterfield [2003] yield many examples. Their work in Indigenous innovations has been highly scrutinized and verified with supporting primary resources.) Most people (often including Indigenous communities) were denied the right to learn this knowledge because of external factors (e.g., colonialism, residential schools, cultural genocide, creation of reserves, inferior policies, racist laws on patenting). This unfortunate history has been instrumental in limiting authentic sharing and relationships between non-Indigenous and Indigenous groups (Dion, Johnston, and Rice 2010).

Indigenous Innovation Areas for Secondary-School Course(s) Inclusion	
	English: languages (oral, written, symbolic, sign), communication techniques, storytelling, legends, education systems/strategies
	Math: astronomy, civil engineering, currency, physical structures, base systems (4, 7, 20, other), tool functions, scales, calendars
	Science: agricultural techniques, domesticated animals, environmental science, zoned biodiversity
	History: architecture, economics, trade, military science, politics, social science, trade, treaties
	Geography: inventions, metallurgy, mapping, environmental knowledge, land connections, weather expertise
	Health: dentistry, foods, nutrition, personal hygiene, pharmacology, medical knowledge and techniques
	Physical Education: carpentry, fishing, aquaculture, hunting, toys, games, sports, transportation, psychology
	Integrated Arts: visual art, clothing, footwear, music, ceramics, fibres, dyes, weaving, tools, toys, drama and theatre

Figure 1.4. *Indigenous Innovation Areas for Secondary-School Course(s) Inclusion. This model is based upon the comprehensive research and series from Keoke and Porterfield (2003). These areas provide the foundation for exploring Indigenous innovations.*

First Nations, Métis, and Inuit peoples in Canada and related cultural regions have given many material and non-material gifts to the world. See if you can identify some of these in your own life:

- laminated bow
- crampon
- dogsled
- flotation device
- home insulation
- kayak
- parka
- shovel
- snow goggles
- portable space heater
- trousers
- anesthetics
- axe
- beans
- box
- bunk bed
- canoe
- caramel corn
- chewing gum
- corn disposable diaper
- fertilizer
- fringed clothing
- hockey
- hair conditioner
- lacrosse
- maple sugar
- mouthwash
- potato chip
- tobacco
- women's rights
- fish hook
- hemostats
- insecticide
- sewing needle
- snack food
- road systems

Important Note! Some of the innovations, such as women's rights and the sewing needle, were also developed independently elsewhere in the world.

This select list is a snapshot into the diversity of innovations that have come from Canada's Indigenous peoples.

This knowledge needs to be told and shared so all people understand and value the real living story of Indigenous peoples (Kanu 2011).

You will find examples of lesson plans, which follow a culturally infused format, in Part 2 (see page 71). These lessons model the pedagogy discussed in this chapter, with adaptations for grades 9 to 12. Each lesson is subject-specific, but you can adapt it to a variety of levels within each grade.

Chapter 2.

INDIGENOUS SELF-ESTEEM AND MENTAL-HEALTH ACTIVITIES

The Twins – *Bimaadziwin* and *Windigos*

Balance, interconnectedness, self-worth, respect, acceptance, support networks, and vision for the future are critical to Indigenous self-esteem (Burack et al. 2014). Today's Indigenous youth face comprehensive challenges. These challenges are represented in Indigenous cultures as *windigos*. Where I live, windigos are the living spirits/forces that are teachers to us all. Windigos are those darker beings like fear, greed, jealousy, anger, hate, and confusion that manifest themselves in the way of addictions, suicides, vandalism, self-loathing, and other illnesses affecting the soul. Windigos can be very painful educators and stagnate the growth of youth who are not informed or equipped to deal with them. Windigos are very real, and our youth face a daily battle with them. We have all faced these forces, and, if we think back to our own days of adolescence, we can relate to the power of these spirits. Young people are seeking both their place and their identities. It will take the concerted effort of a community to guide them in a good way. It is the responsibility of all people to be a guide and light for our youth as they walk the path and journey that we already have (Gollan and Malin 2012).

In traditional societies, every individual had a role in the community. All beings were valued and supported. Each person's ability to fulfill his or her role (e.g., teacher, hunter, warrior, medicine person) affected the wellness and survival of everyone else. The technological age and the effects of colonialism have severely altered traditional societies by disconnecting family structures (Rainbow Schools 2013). Before colonialism, familial units provided strong support to our culture, language, teachings, traditions, and networks for sustenance (Deer 2013a). The impacts of colonialism have been far-reaching and can still be seen in the intergenerational struggles that affect Indigenous peoples. Our youth exhibit both the symptoms and results of this history. On the reserve on the north shores of Lake Huron in northern Ontario where I grew up, I have seen and experienced the impacts firsthand. The power of history is very real, but I believe the resilience of Indigenous peoples is even more powerful.

Balance is key. Balance – and transparency – in all things is critical to the positive self-esteem and mental health of our youth. Naming the issues and identifying the sources in a respectful and nonjudgmental way are important. Blaming and shaming people, outside forces, agencies, and others are the surest ways to remain stuck and stagnant. Our youth need to know the story of colonialism and cultural genocide. However, while they need to know the history that has affected our Nations, our youth must learn this in a way that offers them methods to cope and move beyond this history (Battiste 2011). To feel hopeful, they need a balance of dark and light. Without this balance, our youth will feel anger and may experience unresolved or misguided thoughts and actions. Anger is the seed for confusion and a platform for lack of conscience. Our communities are in a time of cultural resurgence, and our youth are at the centre of this search and reclamation of our lands and rights (Baxter 2006). They and future generations will be entrusted with the legacy of our people. To move forward, we need to be able to look back with an open mind.

Bimaadziwin (the good life) is a sacred journey based on lived teachings that are contemporary and applicable to today (Toulouse 2007). Our youth need to see examples of these teachings and identify with them. Our youth also need to see that for each good-life teaching there exists a darker twin (windigo) that is also very real. This examination of the teachings, and acceptance of them, is the beginning to balance. Understanding there is a fine line between them is also important. Having our youth participate in activities and critical conversations about where they see bimaadziwin and windigos in the world (locally, provincially, nationally, internationally) provide real opportunities for change (Deer 2013b). Knowing the forces our spirits feed will result in thoughts and actions of similar energy. If we continually focus on fear, it will consume our lives and the way we participate in the world and with others. It is critical to understand the many faces of the windigos; however, it is equally important to highlight the lighter twin (with a focused conversation on the lived experiences and examples of these teachings). Parts of these discussions and activities also need to concentrate on the quality of life (physical, emotional, intellectual, and spiritual) that is the direct result of following these light/dark forces (see figure 2.1).

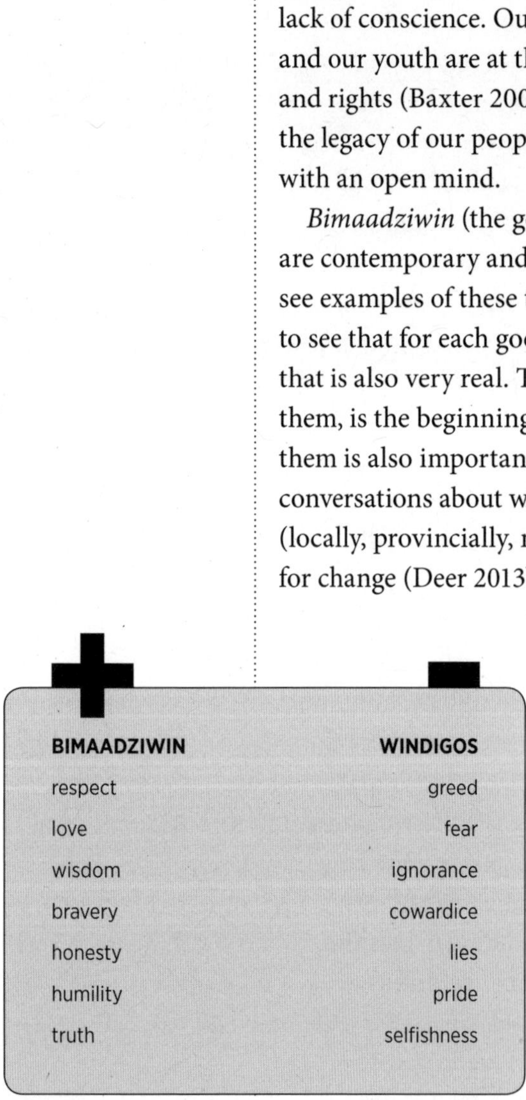

Figure 2.1. *The Twins. This model is based upon the teachings of the Ojibwe. The teachings are known as "the twins" (light and dark). Knowing these teachings is critical to our youth understanding the twins' power today.*

Secondary-School Teaching Strategies on Bimaadziwin/Windigos

Here are some strategies you can use with all students to help them further understand the concepts of bimaadziwin and windigos:

- Establish a relationship of trust and authentic care/concern first.
- Start with neutral and safe topics before moving to heavier personal ones. This process is necessary for establishing a space for comfortable dialogue. For instance, have students research a variety of sources (e.g., newspaper, television, social media, websites) for international, national, and provincial examples of the teachings in action. This becomes the first step in working toward the middle, which is the self.
- Invite dynamic guest speakers, who have overcome struggles, into the classroom. Speakers close to your students' generation or who come from a pop-culture environment provide students with excellent tools for reflection.
- Participate, as a class, in an arts-based multimedia workshop where students depict the teachings. Celebrate these achievements with a gallery showing to honour the interpretations.
- Create a photo journal of images that depicts the teachings. Encourage students to provide captions below each photo capturing their interpretations.
- Set up a speaker's corner for students to share their understanding of the teachings. A speaker's corner gives students the opportunity to address the entire class (either in person or filmed previously).
- Research the science of energy and the physiological realities of windigos to provide an interesting lens for students to debate the existence and power of windigos (e.g., stress, addiction, global warming, suicide, war, cutting, gaming). For example, gaming involves screen time, and most games have violent imagery. Students could research the effects of gaming (increased screen time) on their bodies and the impacts that violent imagery has on this (potential desensitization).
- Examine social issues from a mathematical perspective to provide insights into the effects of these teachings (e.g., statistics and potential correlations between poverty, crime, lack of education, at-risk behaviours).
- Analyze musical playlists in terms of images, lyrics, messages, tempo, pitch, and beat, and relate this to emotional/cultural impacts (e.g., How does it address the treatment of people? What activities does it promote? How is the subconscious being affected? Why is this (not) an important activity to engage in?).

The move toward a full understanding of the self can occur only when respectful protocols for conversations and activities have been explicit and practised in the more neutral areas of dialogue (Government of Ontario 2013). The windigos that exist close to home and the self will be difficult to address, as they are being directly analyzed and/or challenged. Educators need to remember windigos will use many tactics to survive (e.g., denial, withdrawal, confrontation, apathy, avoidance, excuses, pride). This is why support networks for our youth are necessary. These networks ensure growth and the journey of bimaadziwin can take place (Youth Development Committee 2012).

National Resources and Wise Practices

There are many resources and wise practices across Canada that can facilitate the nurturing of self-esteem and discussion of holistic conceptions of mental health. Key organizations and documents are available to educators who are seeking culturally appropriate materials and strategies. The names of the organizations and the titles of the document are organized by province or territory (see figure 2.2). Since website addresses and contact information can change over the years, I highly suggest educators use a search engine of choice to locate these suggested resources when the time arises. This makes accessing these documents and personnel more seamless and current.

Positive self-esteem requires a balance of the physical, spiritual, emotional, and intellectual aspects of the self (best start/meilleur depart 2011). It is through understanding the interconnections of these aspects that critical insights can facilitate transformative change. This process requires meaningful teachings and an interactive analysis of the current state of the self. This is a difficult but rewarding undertaking that places our youth (and ourselves) in a position to get a real picture of where we are, who we are, and the potential for where we can go. This represents only part of a curriculum at the secondary-school level committed to the integration of mental-health knowledge. Every province and territory has identified youth mental health and self-esteem as priorities. Schools have become one of the relevant spaces to facilitate these activities. However, for Indigenous youth the approaches need to be grounded in models that support and bridge a connection to culture (Toulouse 2013).

The following figures from Statistics Canada (2014) make up a distinct profile of Indigenous youth (IY) in Canada:

- IY under the age of 14 make up 28 percent of the total Indigenous population.
- IY aged 15 to 24 represent 18.2 percent of the total Indigenous population.
- Suicide and self-inflicted injuries are the leading cause of death for IY.
- Suicide rates for Inuit youth are the highest in the world.

Alberta	Organizations: Native Counselling Services of Alberta; Project of Heart Document: Mental Health Matters Tools/Resources
British Columbia	Organizations: First Nations Education Steering Committee; here to help, Mental health and substance use information you can trust Document: Mental Health First Aid Courses/Resources
Manitoba	Organizations: Communities That Care (CTC Manitoba); Teen Talk North Manitoba Document: Mental Health Promotion in Schools
New Brunswick	Organizations: First Nation Education Initiative Inc.; Mi'kmaq Maliseet Nations News Document: Canadian Mental Health New Brunswick Education and Training Resources
Newfoundland and Labrador	Organizations: Innu Nation; The Inuit of Nunatsiavut; Qalipu Mi'kmaq First Nation; Combined Councils of Labrador Document: Mental Health and Addictions Clinicians and School District Contact Information
Northwest Territories	Organizations: Akaitcho FN; Dehcho FN; Gwich'in Tribal Council; Inuvialuit Regional Corporation; NWT Métis Nation; Sahtu Secretariat; Tlicho Government Document: A Shared Path Towards Wellness
Nova Scotia	Organizations: The Confederacy of Mainland Mi'kmaq; NADACA, Eskasoni, Mi'Kmaq Document: Teen Mental Health Resources
Nunavut	Organizations: Nunavut Department of Health; I Respect Myself Document: Youth Suicide Prevention Curriculum
Ontario	Organizations: Ontario Native Education Counselling Association; Aboriginal Health Access Centres Document: Supporting Minds, An Educators' Guide to Promoting Students Mental Health & Well-Being
Prince Edward Island	Organizations: Mi'Kmaq Confederacy of Prince Edward Island; Abegweit First Nation Mi'kmaq Wellness Centre Document: CMHA Mental Health High School Curriculm Guide
Quebec	Organizations: First Nations Education Council; First Nations of Quebec and Labrador Health and Social Services Commission Document: Centres of Excellence - LEARN Tool-kits for Teachers
Saskatchewan	Organizations: Indigenous Peoples' Health Research Centre; Aboriginal Friendship Centres of Saskatchewan Document: A Comprehensive School Community Health Approach Resources
Yukon	Organizations: Yukon Native Language Centre; Council of Yukon First Nations Document: reality rules! resources

Figure 2.2. *Resources and Wise Practices. This resource list provides a starting point for finding culturally relevant self-esteem and mental-health materials and services in Canada's provinces and territories.*

- IY are the highest at-risk when it comes to the social determinants of health (e.g., economics, education, quality of relationships).
- Unemployment rates for IY are twice as high as rates for non-IY in the western provinces.
- Twenty-three percent of IY are classified as early school leavers and have not completed secondary school or an equivalency.
- IY who live on-reserve are accused of homicide and break and enter at rates of 11 times and 7 times more than non-IY.

These alarming figures require immediate action from the different spheres within our communities (e.g., educational, social, political, financial) to address the core causes at the heart of these statistics. Education is only one of the key forums to facilitate addressing these issues (Greer et al. 2011).

Mental health and self-esteem are connected. Mental health affects the whole self. When a person suffers from a mental illness, it is important to name the illness, educate to reduce the stigma, have access to the necessary supports, and provide a lens for moving forward in a positive way (Government of Ontario 2013).

Some Indigenous peoples believe there are seven stages in the life of a human being: the good life (birth to 7), the fast life (7 to 14), the wandering/wondering life (14 to 21), the stages of truth life (21 to 28), the planting/planning life (28 to 35), the doing life (35 to 49), and the giving back life (49 onward) (best start/meilleur depart 2011).

> ***Important Note!***
> **Indigenous peoples are diverse in their languages, traditions, and beliefs. This is why it is critical to have a relationship with local nations. The seven stages of life is a teaching within particular nations; for example, the Anishinaabe have the seven stages of life, and the Hindu also have a similar teaching.**

In high school, our youth are at the end of the fast life and entering the wandering/wondering stage. The cultural characteristics of this latter stage are to challenge, question, test limits, and seek new experiences and teachers. The term "teenage brain," as it is often referred to in psychology/physiology, is a pivotal phase in the development of identity. It is also the most difficult to traverse. The relevant supports and influences for our youth determine how they live (and often cope) during this time (Gollan and Malin 2012).

Creating a Living Profile With Students

The creation of a living profile is a long-term process students integrate throughout their semester or revisit throughout their secondary-school career. A living profile requires students' reflections on the teachings from the domains in the wheel of life (see figure 2.3). The purpose of this living profile is for students to investigate the self and identify personal strengths and challenges. This level of reflection can be drawn upon as a tool for personal self-esteem, leadership examination, or career direction. As part of this living profile, it is critical we educate our youth on the stages of life and the factors that affect the whole person. Engaging in a multitude of activities that explore

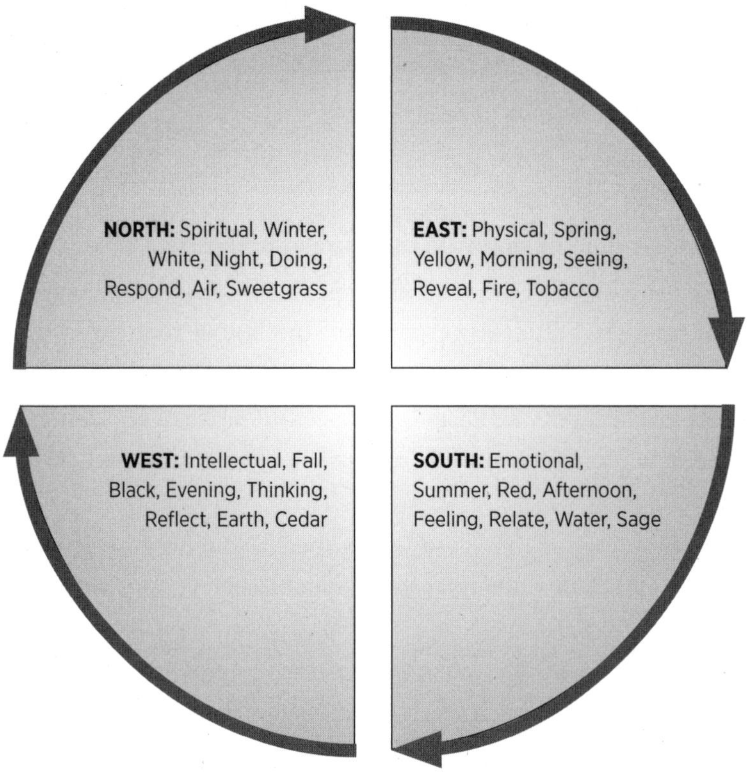

Figure 2.3. *Wheel of Life. This model represents select Ojibwe land-based teachings on living a good life. It is a tool for analyzing the self and a person's areas of strength and growth.*

the wheel of life in their own lives is important to contemporize the teachings and make connections (see figure 2.3).

The living profile is an activity students complete during class with their teachers or during sessions with a guidance counsellor. Students will maintain four folders that are labelled "East," "South," "West," and "North." Each folder will contain personalized activities completed by the students as taught by the teacher or guidance counsellor. The personalized activities should complement the teacher or guidance counsellor's existing in-class or small-group instruction strategies. The living profile is meant to be a place of discovery for students and is not meant to be onerous for educators. For example, if a teacher decides to respectfully revise the teachings into sentence stems for students, or a guidance counsellor decides to create visual organizers with the teachings (respectfully copied), then this is suitable.

It is important to acknowledge that teachers and guidance counsellors come to the classroom with their own set of gifts in terms of experience and teaching strategies. This is highly valued and critical to this process of creating a living profile with students. In terms of a plan to create the living profile with students, the following flexible schedule of ideas is offered:

- Meet with the student or students.
- Label the folders, and share the purpose of the living profile.
- Begin with introductions to each other.
- Share the teachings of The Thirteen Moons and The Four Colours from the Wheel of Life Teachings.
- Have students respond orally on these initial teachings.
- Share the teachings of The East with a specific emphasis on Spring, Yellow, and Morning. Have students respond in a method of your choice and place into folder.
- Share the teachings of The East with a specific emphasis on Seeing, Reveal, Fire, and Tobacco. Have students respond in a method of your choice and place into folder.
- Share the teachings of The South with a specific emphasis on Summer, Red, and Afternoon. Have students respond in a method of your choice and place into folder.
- Share the teachings of The South with a specific emphasis on Feeling, Relate, Water, and Sage. Have students respond in a method of your choice and place into folder.
- Share the teachings of The West with a specific emphasis on Fall, Black, and Evening. Have students respond in a method of your choice and place into folder.
- Share the teachings of The West with a specific emphasis on Thinking, Reflect, Earth, and Cedar. Have students respond in a method of your choice and place into folder.
- Share the teachings of The North with a specific emphasis on Winter, White, and Night. Have students respond in a method of your choice and place into folder.
- Share the teachings of The North with a specific emphasis on Doing, Respond, Air, and Sweetgrass. Have students respond in a method of your choice and place into folder.
- Have students further reflect by examining their four folders with these questions as the springboard:
  - What strengths do I possess?
  - What are areas of challenge?
  - How can I be supported?
  - How am I unique?
  - From the information in the folders, where am I headed? Why (or why not) is this important to know?

- The final stage is to discuss the findings with a community of learners who are supportive (Burack et al. 2014; Youth Development Committee 2012). Depending upon the group dynamics, you may choose a variety of ways to facilitate this critical conversation (e.g., circle, jigsaw, think/pair/share, speaker's corner, poster presentation, creation of webinar, conferencing).

Wheel of Life Teachings

The Thirteen Moons

According to Anishinaabe tradition, the moon is our grandmother. Grandmother Moon has many teachings to share, which she does through her 13 moons. The 13 moons of the Anishinaabe calendar are defined by the time of the year each occurs. The four seasons, represented on the living wheel by the four directions, have unique moons defined by 28-day cycles and activities in nature that occur during those cycles. In spring, for example, Sugar Moon occurs when the preparations for the sugar bush begin. The moon that follows, Sucker Moon, represents the running of the sucker, which happens during the next moon phase.

The Four Colours

On the wheel of life, four colours represent Ojibwe understandings of the beginning of time and the people who exist on the earth. All people can be found somewhere on this wheel – either through their season of birth or from a teaching that compels them to further study the self. It is said the Creator gave each race inherent gifts to share with everyone.

East

The east represents the physical aspect of the self. This is where we explore those things related to our body; body mass index, nutrition (including snack foods), liquid intake (including caffeine and/or alcohol), activity levels/sedentary levels, and sleep (times and quality). From this information, we assess areas of strength and areas for change. The east also provides youth a space for the exploration of these teachings:

- Spring – This season represents a time of new growth and new beginnings. It is known by three moons: Sugar Moon, Sucker Moon, Flower Moon. The Sugar Moon represents a time of family and a cleansing of the negative forces in our lives. The Sucker Moon represents the sucker fish, which can survive in any body of water. The sucker fish does its part in the world by cleaning the waters of the pollutants humans leave behind. The Flower Moon represents new energies and diversity everywhere. It is a celebration of the beauty in all things Mother Earth has provided.

- Yellow – The colour yellow is seen in the land of the Ojibwe in many forms (e.g., yellow birch, the sun, flowers, medicines). People from this area of the living wheel are known for their ideas, innovativeness, and strong observance of traditional protocols.
- Morning – This represents a time of thankfulness. The sun rises and greets us to start a new day. It is a time of preparation for all the experiences we will have. How we rise and the spirit in which we do influence our thoughts and actions.
- Seeing – This aspect of the living wheel refers to a learning style. One way we learn is by seeing. We see with our eyes and with our spirits.
- Reveal – This refers to perspective. It cuts to the core of understanding the true nature of our family, friends, animals, the earth, and other things. It focuses on the acceptance of the uniqueness of each being in our life.
- Fire – This element has many meanings. It represents the power of the sun and the power of magma at the centre of the earth. It is our connection to survival. Fire is so powerful that it can both heal and destroy. It is sacred and refers to the spirit connections we have and those that positively affect us.
- Tobacco – This is a sacred medicine that is to be honoured. Tobacco represents the hard work humans expend to sustain it. It also is used to give thanks to the Creator. It is a guide and a healer.

South

The south represents the emotional aspect of the self. This section identifies all the positive characteristics that encapsulate who we are (e.g., good friend, respectful, good sense of humour, awesome gamer) (Toulouse 2007). This is also where illnesses that impact our lives are located (e.g., anxiety, mood disorder, attention/impulsivity diagnoses, behaviour assessments, eating/weight issues, substance abuse, self-harm). It is where we identify the forces – people and influences – in our lives. Each person and influence must be correlated with a set of key words that describes our relationship with them and their impacts upon us. The south gives youth an opportunity to list the social activities they are interested or engaged in (e.g., hobbies, interests, jobs, roles, favourite music, favourite shows). The south also illuminates the following teachings:

- Summer – This season represents a time of fullness and growth. All beings reach toward the warmth of the skies and celebrate the length of the day. It is known by three moons (Strawberry Moon, Raspberry/Blueberry Moon, Grain Moon). Strawberry Moon is heart berry time. (Heart berry is the English translation of the Ojibwe word *Ode'min*, which is the word applied by Ojibwe people to the strawberry.) Strawberry Moon represents kindness and the celebration of life. Raspberry/Blueberry Moon sets boundaries and overcomes challenges. This moon represents the perseverance and strength of the berries. Grain Moon represents preparation. Harvesting and celebrating the bounty in our lives are located here.

- Red – The colour red is often associated with Indigenous peoples and the gifts they gave to the world, both material and nonmaterial, especially the gifts of friendship and humour. Red can be seen everywhere in nature in Ojibwe country (e.g., red maple, peppermint berry, robin, medicine).
- Afternoon – The sun is at its fullest during this time of the day. We are often engaged in work, school, or other life and career activities. It is a time of celebrating the potential we possess as human beings.
- Feeling – We learn by feeling. We need to have an emotional connection to a subject to really know it. This is either out of interest or facilitated by a good teacher.
- Relate – Part of having a holistic perspective is being able to relate to others (e.g., humans, animals, the earth, elements). It is about the interconnectedness of all things.
- Water – Water makes up most of the human body. Water also fills the veins of Mother Earth (e.g., lakes, rivers, streams, oceans, groundwater). Water is powerful and connected to the moon. It can enlighten, and it can destroy. We cannot survive without water. It our responsibility to protect it.
- Sage – This is a powerful medicine that cleanses negativity. When used in smudges, it clears spaces (human, spirit) of harmful energies and provides clarity of thought.

West

The west represents the intellectual aspect of the self. This is the place where we identify our education, career goals, and steps toward achievement. It is also where we articulate the potential blocks to achievement (e.g., poverty, health, violence, peers). Identifying the challenges is critical, as the other side of this activity is identifying solutions and known sources of support to combat them. The west is where teachers, role models, researchers, guidance counsellors, parents, guardians, Elders, and other resources are pivotal (Greer et al. 2011; Rainbow Schools 2013). The west also provides youth with a space for the exploration of these teachings:

- Fall – This season represents reflection and change. It has three moons: Corn Moon, Falling Leaves Moon, Freezing Moon. Corn Moon encompasses the teachings of all 13 moons, and each kernel represents the distinctiveness of every being on Earth. Each kernel and each row coexists in harmony. Falling Leaves Moon occurs when Mother Earth puts on her most colourful dress for us. She shows us how much she loves us and all of her children by dressing Ojibwe lands in leaves of reds, yellows, oranges, and browns. Freezing Moon represents dreaming. It is when the stars are prominent in the skies and seem closer to the earth than at any other time of the year. Fall is a time of visions and of seeing anything is possible.

- Black – This colour is represented by the legend of rainbow crow. A crow is classified as black in colour; however, if you look at the crow in the sun you will see all colours of the spectrum. People in this domain or those who have roots in this part of the living wheel have limitless creativity and strength of voice.
- Evening – At this time of day, the sun begins its journey to meet Grandmother Moon. According to the Ojibwe, the moon is our grandmother. Grandmother moon has many teachings to share, which she does through the annual calendar of 13 moons. A space is provided to acknowledge our contributions and the gifts, and to give thanks for the experiences in the day (i.e., negative and positive teach us something about ourselves and can promote action).
- Thinking – We learn by being engaged in thinking activities that challenge our minds. It is one of the many ways we personalize knowledge.
- Reflect – A healthy world-view is having the ability to reflect. Reflection also requires action on our parts to contribute to the light of the world.
- Earth – We cannot survive without her. She is our mother. This aspect of the teachings has us thinking about the seven generations yet to come (i.e., looking at our environmental footprint).
- Cedar – This is a medicine that can be converted into many things: tea to get rid of headaches, salve to heal sores, aromatherapy to provide a sense of peace.

North

The north represents the spiritual aspect of the self. This is where we identify the connections we have with other beings of all kinds and of something greater than ourselves (e.g., look for answers to questions such as Why are we here? and What is our purpose?). North also represents the space where each youth creates a life map that documents his or her journey of influence in the world (Battiste 2011). A life map is a *sketch-to-learn* activity whereby students draw out their life as if it were a road map. They start at the beginning (birth) and record monumental events in their lives (e.g., graduations, driver's licence, trips, first concert). The life map requires youth to make predictions for the accomplishments they will have in a long life (to Eldership and beyond). The north also provides youth a space for the exploration of these teachings:

- Winter – This season represents deep introspection and connecting with ancestors. There are four moons in this season: Little Spirit Moon, Big Spirit Moon, Spirit Moon, Bear Moon. Little Spirit Moon is the beginning of a focused inner journey. It represents the spark that lights our sacred fires. Big Spirit Moon represents the path toward purification. Our inner work is to be done without interference. This means we make the time and find the space to be alone in our thoughts. Spirit Moon represents the teachings of silence and the path of the ancestors. The Northern Lights show us that those who came before us are watching us. Bear Moon represents the power of the bond between a mother bear and her cubs. She knows when to nurture them, when to protect them, and when to let them go.
- White – This colour is associated with the stars, the clouds, the movement of waves, and the manifestation of air. Human beings coming from this domain have been given the gift of adaptation and adventure. They can live in all areas of the world.
- Night –This, traditionally, is the time when we enter the world of dreams and when Grandmother Moon watches over us. It is a space to travel in our minds and to other places. We replenish ourselves in this state of sleeping and dreaming.
- Doing – We learn by doing. Being involved in hands-on activities is a primary way knowledge is retained. Activity is key here.
- Respond – Our perspective provides us with the ability to respond (i.e., we can act or not). When we respond, we are being conscious of how we live and interact with others.
- Air – We cannot live without air. Air is powerful and beautiful. It can destroy (tornadoes) or it can flourish, becoming a wind that carries seeds around the earth. Air comes from our mother, the earth. We can see her breath in the form of fog.
- Sweetgrass – Braided in three to represent mind, body, and spirit, sweetgrass is a medicine that protects. It is a reminder to take care of ourselves so we can help others (e.g., human beings; animals; the elements of water, fire, air, and earth).

Additional Curricular Connections on Mental Health and Self-Esteem Concepts

You can integrate the following curricular connections into your secondary classrooms and adapt them for various grades and levels at your school.

- English – Invite a local Indigenous guest speaker who is known for storytelling. Have a discussion circle about the teachings he or she introduces. This can be done with the speaker present or with the class only.
- Math – Attend a public Indigenous celebration, and photograph (with permission from the participants) regalia. Document the geometry, angles, and symbology at the celebration.
- Science – In collaboration with a local Indigenous resource person, go on a medicine walk in the area. Keep a learning log of plants, their properties, and their applications.
- History – Create a graffiti wall featuring the contributions of Indigenous peoples and historical facts about them. Create a speaker's corner where students can honour each other.
- Geography – Participate in a land-based activity that is facilitated by Indigenous peoples of the area. This is ideally planned in line with the seasonal activities of the Indigenous peoples of your area. Have students create a collage of teachings from the activity.
- Music – Locate Indigenous music from a variety of genres (e.g., rap, flute, classical, traditional, country, alternative). This is further described as music from Indigenous musicians, lyrics that reflect Indigenous themes/topics, music based on Indigenous melodies/rhythms, and music that uses traditional Indigenous instruments. Analyze the messages and effects.
- Drama – View a drama series or play written or produced by Indigenous peoples. Use the jigsaw method to highlight the issues, themes, and personal connections that are illuminated.
- Visual Arts – Bring in a local Indigenous craftsperson or artist. You may want to visit his or her studio or workshop. Back in the classroom, create an adaptation of that craft that integrates symbols of the students' gifts to the world.
- Career Studies – Research opportunities to work with Indigenous peoples locally, provincially, nationally, and globally. Focus on areas of personal aptitude.
- Business and Technology – Collaborate with an Indigenous secondary-school class or organization, and develop a business plan that incorporates social action.

***Important Note!* Going out to the sugar bush or on a medicine walk with an Elder is an example of a land-based activity.**

***Important Note!* The Project of Heart organization partners schools with Indigenous communities in an inquiry-based process to learn about the effects of residential schools and other social issues. Each partnership varies in its outcomes and social-justice results.**

Chapter 3.

DIFFERENTIATED INSTRUCTION AND BLOOM'S TAXONOMY

Differentiated Instruction

Differentiated Instruction (DI) complements Indigenous world-view and pedagogical methods in education (Steinhardt School of Culture, Education, and Human Development 2008; Toulouse 2013). Our youth in secondary schools require DI to have success, find meaning, and become engaged with their subjects. DI is based upon educators embracing change in the content (readiness), the process (interests), the product (based on learning profiles), and the learning environment (conditions for learning) (Ontario Ministry of Education 2010). Balance, diversity, and tasks that creatively engage the mind are necessary to engagement and student success.

So, what does DI look like? How can you begin planning DI in your courses? Why is DI so important to the success of Indigenous students? Why is DI critical to all your students? Teachers are faced with new policies, programs, updates, changes, testing, and accountability measures on a daily basis. This reality can be overwhelming, and educators need time, resources, and accessible professional development to meet these challenges head on (Northey 2005). I have been to many sessions where the facilitator talks for hours about DI and not once shows me or engages me in ways to implement DI. I have been to even more sessions where I am given statistics about the attrition rates of Indigenous youth and those deemed at-risk, but I am rarely provided with tangible ways as a practitioner to work with our youth. In my teaching practice, I implement DI by:

- discovering the learning styles of my students
- using diverse strategies for teaching, learning and assessment, and evaluation
- starting where my students are at
- offering choice
- taking a tiered approach to content (i.e., scaffolding)

DI integrates learning and assessment and facilitates student ownership of their knowledge. The focus is on students' achievements, their learning needs, and the comprehension and demonstration of provincial/territorial curricular outcomes.

Although DI facilitates student success and engagement, it also has to be manageable, organized, and introduced on a continuum (Gregory and Herndon 2010). It requires the educator to create a planned sequence of gradual release of responsibility to the student. The skills to create a sustained environment of DI in secondary schools need to be taught. Teachers may begin by introducing various teaching methods (first, from inside their own comfort zone, such as inside the classroom; later, from outside this comfort zone, participating in, for example, outside activities) and then providing options for students to demonstrate their learning (Johnson 2013). The next stage of this process is to have instruction, assessment, and evaluation practices that complement the learning styles of the students. As the final evolution of DI, I also think it is critical to introduce activities that challenge traditional ways students demonstrate their learning (e.g., tests, reports). For example, inviting students to share their own ideas of assessment (formative and summative) is key. The use of more creative and critical thinking tools such as portfolios of learning, photo montages, cultural performances (e.g., drumming, dance) and other alternative forms of evaluation are valued.

DI is about how the teacher plans activities and assessment and evaluation in the content (curriculum/subject matter and student readiness), the process (instructional strategies), the product (the output or material demonstration of the curricular expectations), and the learning environment, including structure of classroom and learning space(s).

The Content

In a DI model, content, as reflected in the curriculum expectations, must be evaluated against a student's basic understanding of the subject matter and his or her readiness to build on existing knowledge (Ontario Ministry of Education 2010). It is the students' level of comfort and understanding with the subject matter that the teacher is presenting (e.g., Indigenous authors, treaties, self-determination, First Nations' rights). Begin by doing a pre-assessment of students' knowledge in the area of study. Based upon this evidence, some of the ways secondary teachers can differentiate the subject content are by offering the following (Johnson 2013):

- mini-lessons with a variety of visual organizers and scaffolding activities
- choices in books, texts, and other media
- multiple-level questioning
- webquests, virtual field trips, online scavenger hunts
- problem-based learning and inquiry models
- mini-workshops aimed at reteaching and/or extending knowledge
- labs, stations, centres, simulations

- independent studies and open-ended activities
- jigsaw, carousel, and other cooperative teaching methods

The Process

Process involves including students' interests in the topic and using a variety of instructional methods for different types of learners (Gregory and Herndon 2010). Some ways secondary educators can differentiate the learning process are (Northey 2005):

- think/pair/share or think/pair/block
- flexible seating and interest groupings
- teams, games, and tournaments
- literature circles and R.A.F.T. exercises
- mini-workshops and mini-lessons using a variety of technology (e.g., Prezi, PPT)
- learning contracts and goal setting
- cubing and tiered assignments
- varied journal, questions, and sentence prompts
- mentors and reading buddies
- independent studies and centres (folders with a variety of learning activities focused on core content)
- group investigations (with clarity of roles)

The Product

Product refers to the student output of curricular expectations. Product reflects the application of knowledge and ways students respond to and show what they have learned (Johnson 2013). Different students may have different ways of showing learning (Ontario Ministry of Education 2010). Final products include:

- reports
- quizzes
- collages
- lyrics
- poetry
- book talks
- journals
- videos
- blogs
- social-media platforms
- software applications
- magazines
- storytelling
- model making
- graphing
- case studies
- experiments
- technical designs
- Q & As
- problem-based models
- learning logs

The Learning Environment

The learning environment refers to the structure, space, materials, groupings, and classroom-management techniques employed (e.g., asking questions, confirming learning, using technology in the classroom) (Northey 2005). Some of the ways secondary educators can differentiate their learning environments are by (Johnson 2013):

- changing student groupings (e.g., pairs, amoebas, inner/outer circles, carousel, jigsaw)
- altering the seating (e.g., flexible, circle, rows, small groups, u-shape)
- offering multiple learning points in the classroom (e.g., video, word walls, problem cards, stations with folders/Ziplocs, speaker's corners, audio-mp3 players, laptops with headphones, projection, Smart boards)
- integrating field trips (live and virtual) and events (live and virtual)
- accessing other school spaces and resources (library, language lab, courtyard, gymnasium, planetarium)
- introducing new learning materials in the class (manipulatives, books, video, music, timelines, equipment, centres)

Examples of a DI Continuum Using Indigenous Content

Figure 3.1 highlights how Indigenous content and current issues in secondary English and History/Civics classes are represented in a progression (DI continuum).

Another way secondary-school teachers can differentiate learning opportunities for students with a focus on Indigenous content is by exploring ideas in relevant subject areas (Aboriginal Literacy Foundation 2012):

- Math – Research and collect Indigenous calendars from around the world (e.g., 13 moons, Mayan). Document the numerical and spatial differences from Gregorian calendars. Highlight the geometrical intricacies of each of these calendars. Students select a preferred presentation method of findings.
- Science – Investigate the theories (teachings) and examples of "the environmental footprint" as understood by Indigenous peoples around the world. Analyze the complexities, similarities, and differences between them. Connect to current movements in environmental stewardship. Students select a preferred product for presentation.
- Geography – Highlight the terrains and ecosystems Indigenous peoples live or lived in around the world. Identify the innovations that evolved from these distinctive relationships with the land. Students roll the cube (which identifies an assortment of products to complete for a lesson) and select one to pursue. Examples of products are the creation of maps, dioramas, research reports, and iMovies to document the learning.

***Important Note!* The Métis have the "Sacred Act of Living a Good Life" teaching that is represented in the form of a tree. One of the four main branches represents the preservation of the land, and this is directly connected to the actions of the self, all people, and the traditions.**

English Class

- **Level 1 DI:** Listen to Wab Kinew's rap "Heroes." Complete an exit card on key learning(s).
- **Level 2 DI:** Listen to Wab Kinew's rap "Heroes." Over five classes, complete a collage, discussion, mini-report, list, and letter on key learning(s).
- **Level 3 DI:** Listen to, view video, and/or read the lyrics of Wab Kinew's rap "Heroes." Students have a choice of many activities (folders with a variety of activity options).
- **Level 4 DI:** Listen to, view video, and/or analyze the lyrics of Wab Kinew's rap "Heroes." Based on learning contracts with students, have them pursue a theme, concept, and/or message. Each student then selects a method to represent the key learning(s).

History/Civics Class

- **Level 1 DI:** Complete the anticipation guide for the viewing of *Kanehsatake: 270 Years of Resistance.* Discuss.
- **Level 2 DI:** View *Kanehsatake* in sections. For each segment, complete one of the following as a class: placemat, jigsaw, time line, mind map, and reflection.
- **Level 3 DI:** Explore three media on the OKA crisis. Students have a choice of R.A.F.T.s,[1] centres – online and cubes (with activity and themed options).
- **Level 4 DI:** Assess the impact of the OKA crisis on a variety of beings and levels. Develop a plan (with clear success criteria) for pursuing further analysis of the topic. Identify a method for representation. Justify the choice by linking back to or modifying success criteria.

Figure 3.1. *Incorporating Indigenous Content into a Differentiated Instruction Continuum. This model represents the DI continuum in two secondary courses that incorporate Indigenous content (Level 1 is least DI and Level 4 is most DI).*

- Music – Listen to a variety of music genres that feature Indigenous artists (e.g., rap, classical, flute, contemporary, pop) through at least three media (e.g., videos, online, live recordings). Students can pursue a genre, a theme, an artist, a region, a time period, or a musical feature (e.g., instrumentation, tone, pitch) to research and present, or play on an instrument.
- Drama – Conduct a table read of a play by Drew Hayden Taylor, an Ojibwe writer, or another Indigenous playwright. Identify the themes that emerge from the content. Students select a theme to pursue and create a storyboard, a video, a commercial, a one-act follow up, a series of role-plays, and/or a mock interview that illustrates this Indigenous issue. Examples are the themes of clashing cultures and substance abuse, which are found in Taylor's "Only Drunks and Children Tell the Truth." The story applies to the lives of today's youth.
- Visual Arts – Plan a social justice and arts action project that builds relationships with Indigenous youth. Connect with a community through your Indigenous lead, Native counsellor, or local friendship centre. The

1 R.A.F.T. refers to a literacy technique that is applied across subject areas. R means Role of the Writer, A means Audience, F means Format, T means Topic.

format for this project is collectively decided by the group (students, teachers, Indigenous community) with possible examples provided (e.g., graffiti walls, photography, exhibitions, chalk-art mini-festival).

- Health and Physical Education – Provide students with a series of resources on Indigenous games from around the world (GoodMinds, a company in Oshweken, Ontario, is a good source for Indigenous books and learning materials). Facilitate the playing of these games (e.g., footbags aka hacky sacks, field hockey, ring toss). Organize a mini-tournament of these games with a focus on the physiology and skills required. Students select games and create the presentations (choice).
- Business Studies – Complete advance organizers on the functions and essentials of successful businesses (e.g., marketing, finances, ethics, digital literacy). Go to a local-delivery mechanism that is Indigenous managed or Indigenous centred. Locate information on an Indigenous business that is of interest. Analyze the business using the advance organizer, or interview the proprietor using the information (with an emphasis on unique business practices). Present findings using a method of choice.
- Technology – Create a respectful online game that highlights the inventions, diversity, and contributions of Indigenous peoples around the world. Students select Nations or areas of interest to pursue and research. A collaborative design process for the online game will be facilitated by the teacher.
- Indigenous Studies – Attend a workshop, conference, or celebration organized by Indigenous peoples in the area. Students can select a method to demonstrate their key learning(s). Plan a classroom gallery walk or exhibition of student work to reflect the teachings of this day.

Bloom's Revised Taxonomy

Bloom's Taxonomy, published in 1948, was created by psychologist Benjamin Bloom (Munzenmaier and Rubin 2013). It was intended as a tool to measure student performance in relation to educational goals and their domains (cognitive, affective, psychomotor). It is one of the most widely applied instruments in education. It also has undergone several revisions over the years to reflect changes in society and schooling. Bloom's Taxonomy complements the teaching/learning styles of Indigenous students, because it is based upon the interconnections between various levels of learning. The revised Bloom's Taxonomy offers a variety of student-centred learning processes and provides secondary educators with visual examples of how this type of pedagogy is achieved (Marzano and Kendall 2007). It offers teacher-friendly illustrations of the potential products and inquiry questions

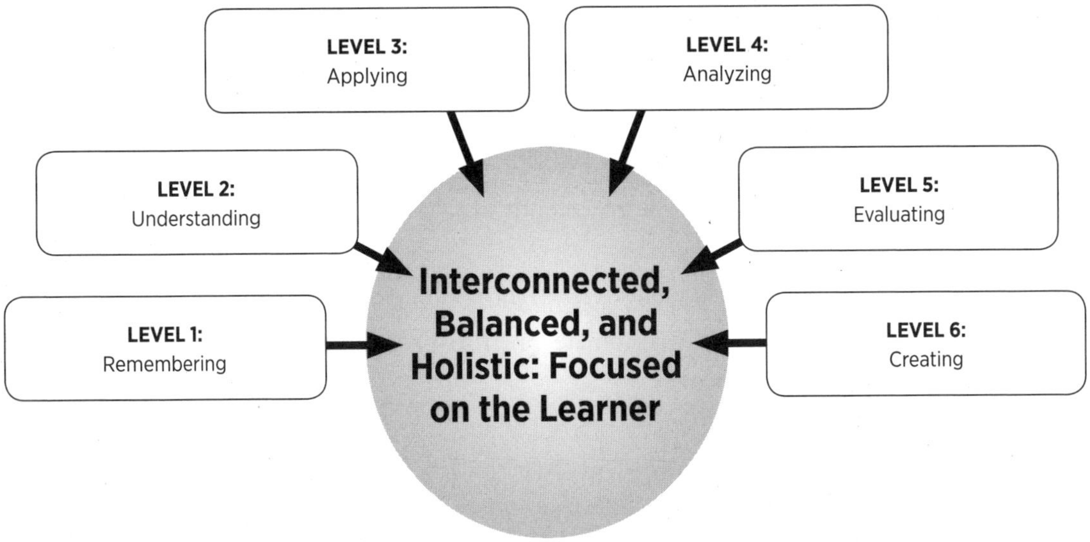

Figure 3.2. *Thinking Continuum Based on Bloom's Revised Taxonomy. This model represents a continuum of lower-order thinking (levels 1 through to 3) and higher-order thinking (levels 4 through to 6). Balance in each is ideal.*

for implementation to aid in course planning. Bloom's Revised Taxonomy is a holistic alternative to consider when targeting more inclusive and complementary Indigenous practices in education (see figure 3.2) (Widdowson and Howard 2013).

Connecting Bloom's Revised Taxonomy to the Ojibwe Living Wheel

The domain of remembering is categorized as Level 1 thinking and focuses on recalling information. It is connected to the physical aspect of the Ojibwe living wheel. This level represents basic knowledge and basic needs.

The domains of understanding (Level 2) and applying (Level 3) are connected to the emotional aspect of the Ojibwe living wheel. These domains involve comprehending new information and applying this new information to unique situations.

The domains of analyzing (Level 4) and evaluating (Level 5) connect with the intellectual aspect of the Ojibwe living wheel. These modes of thinking involve breaking down information and judging the merit of this information. They connect to the intellectual stage of critical thinking that leads to intended action.

The domain of creating (Level 6) is directly related to the spiritual aspect of the Ojibwe living wheel. This stage is highest in the order and reflects engagement with and development of original ideas (Darshana 2014) and holistic-centred knowledge.

Corresponding activities exist for each level of the taxonomy. It is necessary to have a balance of each when planning a learning cycle (unit) for your course(s). Some vocabulary and student-work options secondary-school teachers can incorporate into their subjects are (teachthought 2014):

- Remembering: list, locate, find, name, cite, define, label, listen, choose, relate
  - Student work: quizzes, worksheets (cloze), word searches, fact pages
- Understanding: observe, recognize, calculate, ask, discuss, identify, retell, review
  - Student work: tables, précis, show and tell, journal, blog
- Applying: adapt, manipulate, practise, produce, show, solve, teach, experiment, draw
  - Student work: diary, interview, sculpture, illustration, performance
- Analyzing: diagram, distinguish, group, interpret, order, question, research, classify
  - Student work: mobile, graph, chart, survey, report, checklist
- Evaluating: argue, prioritize, recommend, support, determine, debate, conclude, rate
  - Student work: persuasive speech, panel, debate, investigative report
- Creating: infer, imagine, revise, compose, formulate, show, assemble, design, plan
  - Student work: painting, media project, song, story, film

These represent only a few ways to involve different learners in the classroom. To be successful, Indigenous students require a diverse selection of meaningful activities in their secondary courses.

In appendix A, you will find 13 maps. The first map (see page 153) shows the 12 geographical areas Indigenous peoples live in on Turtle Island (North America and part of the Mesoamericas). It is a topographical classification, not a cultural one. The 12 maps that follow document the 500 Nations that co-exist on Turtle Island. All of the maps originate from the work of Carl Waldman (a famous cartographer) and have been adapted by Keoke and Porterfield (2003) in their series, American Indian Contributions to the World. Appendix B is a reference list (albeit, incomplete) of common names and alternative names of self-identification for Indigenous peoples in Canada and the United States. As always, I highly encourage educators to form relations with local First Nations, Métis, and Inuit communities/organizations in order to access primary resources (e.g., maps, artifacts) (Nicol and Korteweg 2010). However, in the absence of these resources and/or relations, the maps in this book are a good starting point for exploration, using the questions below.

Inquiry questions that can be incorporated into the learning cycles (units) of secondary-school courses are reflected here. These sentence stems originate from the work of Bloom and the revised version of this taxonomy (Marzano and Kendall 2007).

Remembering Questions (Level 1) and the 500 Nations

- What is the important information presented in these maps?
- What are the terms used to identify the geographical features?
- Can you name the Indigenous Nations located in your area?
- How many Indigenous Nations are located in the map related to your area?
- Can you explain why the political borders on these maps are different from those on traditional political maps?

Understanding Questions (Level 2) and the 500 Nations

- What differences exist between these maps and Indigenous Nations?
- Can you write in your own words the significance of these maps and Indigenous names?
- Who do you think you can contact in your area to get a current version of Indigenous populations?
- Can you write a brief outline of the different Indigenous Nations seen on these maps?

Applying Questions (Level 3) and the 500 Nations

- What questions would you ask the Indigenous Nations in your area?
- Would this information (map, Nations, Indigenous names) be more useful if you had a relationship with a local Indigenous Nation?
- Can you group by characteristics other than geography for these Nations?
- From this information given in the text, can you develop a set of instructions about how to navigate these maps and information on these Nations?

Analyzing Questions (Level 4) and the 500 Nations

- What are some of the problems that may be associated with these maps and the listed Nations?
- What were some of the motives behind settlement on Turtle Island by settler cultures?
- What was the turning point in your knowledge about the 500 Nations?
- How is the map of Indigenous Nations in your area similar to today?

Evaluating Questions (Level 5) and the 500 Nations

- How many ways can you connect these maps and Nations to contemporary geographical places/spaces?

- Can you design an organizer to present these many Nations to others?
- How could you compose a song that expresses the diversity of these Nations? Write the lyrics and put the words to music.
- What would happen if these Nations lost their land and/or languages?

Creating Questions (Level 6) and the 500 Nations

- Do you think settlement by non-Indigenous peoples on Turtle Island was a good or a bad thing? Explain your answer.
- How would you have handled things differently with Indigenous peoples?
- Do you believe these 500 Nations co-existed/co-exist harmoniously on Turtle Island? Explain your answer.
- What changes to the maps would you now recommend?

Secondary-school educators who embrace the Bloom's Revised Taxonomy model and draw student work and questions from it will experience more meaningful learner engagement (Nicol and Korteweg 2010). A culturally appropriate version that integrates Ojibwe world-view and the revised Bloom's Taxonomy was introduced at the beginning of this section (see figure 3.2). A more visual presentation of this model is reflected in figure 3.3.

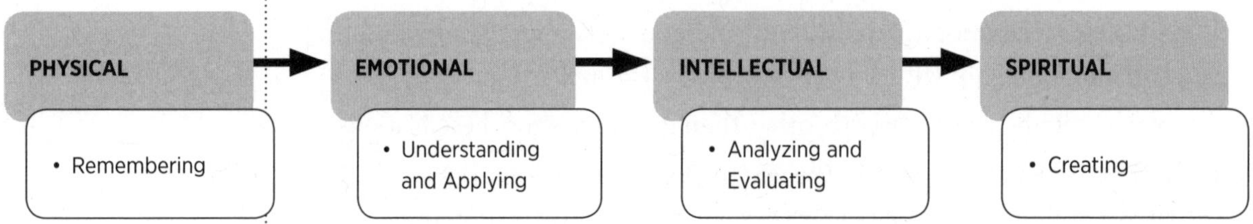

Figure 3.3. *Ojibwe World-view and Bloom's Revised Taxonomy. A balance of activities, questions, and learning outcomes (verb based) from these four areas should be included in any secondary-school course incorporating Indigenous perspectives.*

As stated earlier, DI and Bloom's Revised Taxonomy are pedagogical approaches that support Indigenous learner success in the secondary classroom (Toulouse 2013). Both consider the whole student. Secondary-school teachers can be confident in selecting strategies from both DI and Bloom's Revised Taxonomy as respectful ways to begin (and facilitate) inclusive practices in their courses. However, the applications of DI and Bloom's Revised Taxonomy are only as successful as the resources included in classroom experiences (e.g., learning cycles, lesson plans). Educators need to ensure texts, videos, websites, social media, events, geographical spaces, and other materials are culturally relevant and accurate (Widdowson and Howard 2013). This is why it is so important to have a strong relationship with the Indigenous lead at your school board or with the personnel entrusted with this area of education.

Resources

I am fortunate to work in a province where amazing collaborations have resulted in the creation of secondary-school curriculum documents with an Indigenous focus. The 20 resources listed below are ones I recommend, having used them with my own students. Each resource engages students with authentic Indigenous knowledge and current issues. These resources, combined with DI practices and Bloom's Revised Taxonomy products/ questions, have contributed to the building of community in my own courses. The following resources can be easily found online by typing their titles into a search engine:

- Full Circle: First Nations, Métis, and Inuit Ways of Knowing (Ontario Secondary School Teachers' Federation)
- First Nation, Métis, and Inuit: Tracing Our Historical Footprints – A practical guide to embedding First Nation, Métis, and Inuit Content (York Region District School Board)
- First Nation, Métis, and Inuit Presence in Rainbow Schools (Rainbow District School Board)
- Police MKWA Opportunity Circle (Sudbury Catholic Schools)
- First Peoples Resource Collection – Bundle of First Nation, Métis, and Inuit Materials – Secondary Book Bins (Lakehead Public Schools)
- Secondary Indigenous Education Resource List (Hastings and Prince Edward District School Board)
- Aboriginal Education Strategy. Practical teaching strategies for the secondary classroom (Ontario Ministry of Education)
- Promising Practices in Aboriginal Education – Exemplary classroom practice – Secondary Education (Martin Aboriginal Education Initiative)
- Secondary Resources at GoodMinds.com
- Aboriginal Resources link at the website for the Durham District School Board
- Aboriginal Peoples in Canada (Pearson Canada and GoodMinds)
- Aboriginal Beliefs, Values, and Aspirations (Pearson Canada and GoodMinds)
- First Nation, Métis, and Inuit (FNMI) Education Resources at the Simcoe County District School Board
- Strength and Struggle: Perspectives from First Nations, Inuit, and Métis Peoples in Canada (McGraw-Hill Ryerson)
- Transitions: Supporting First Nations, Inuit, and Métis Students in School and Career Success – website and resources (Ontario Native Education Counselling Association)

- Métis Education Kit (Métis Nation of Ontario)
- Resources from the Inuit Knowledge Centre (Inuit Tapiriit Kanatami)
- Beyond Shadows: First Nations, Métis, and Inuit Student Success (Canadian Teachers' Federation)
- A Truthful Narrative: Bringing First Nations, Métis, and Inuit Contributions to the world into the K–12 curriculum (Education Canada June 2014 Edition)
- CBC News/Aboriginal Website with links and resources, including the series, 8th fire (Canadian Broadcasting Company)

The importance of including members of Indigenous communities and their own experiences, materials, and events cannot be overstated. The impacts of these relationships will further enhance and strengthen the pedagogy inherent in DI and Bloom's Revised Taxonomy. Secondary-school teachers who embrace these resources and teaching strategies (activities and levelled questions) from this chapter will have students leave their courses with a greater appreciation for Indigenous peoples and for themselves (Munzenmaier and Rubin 2013).

Chapter 4.

ATTRITION, RETENTION, TRANSITION, AND GRADUATION CONTINUUM

Attrition

In Canada, Indigenous students have the highest rate of attrition in secondary schools and the lowest rate of graduation. According to the 2010 Labour Force Survey by Usalcas, 22.6 percent of Indigenous youth aged 20 to 24 did not possess a secondary-school diploma. More specifically, 25.8 percent of First Nations youth living off-reserve and 18.9 percent of Métis did not complete high school. The numbers for First Nations youth living on-reserve and Inuit students were considerably higher, and depending upon the area (factors such as remoteness), could represent statistics upwards of 75 percent. Although these statistics have been lowering and there has been an increase in secondary graduation rates, the challenge to retain Indigenous peoples in school is still complex. To fully understand the educational status of Indigenous youth in secondary school, one must examine factors leading to leaving school early and those programs and practices that promote student success (Friesen and Krauth 2012).

Why do Indigenous youth choose to leave secondary school? What can be done to support Indigenous students and facilitate their success in high school? It is important to begin with the reasons that contribute to attrition (Chiefs Assembly on Education 2012; Lamb 2014):

- poverty and related at-risk factors (social determinants of health)
- lack of engagement with subject matter (not culturally meaningful)
- lack of parental/guardian involvement (nonparticipation in school)
- lack of academic preparedness/career planning (limited choice in postsecondary or work-related options)
- mental health/self-esteem issues often intergenerational impact
- few connections to real-life experiences (no relevancy in world-view)
- structural barriers (e.g., racism; marginalization; exclusion by way of policies, programs, people in certain positions)

As educators, we are committed to giving our students equitable access to many opportunities and choices in careers and in life. I believe school planning that focuses on the most at-risk will have the benefit of reaching all students. Such planning also builds relationships and understanding, thus promoting inclusive and respectful communities. Indigenous students face barriers no other group can fully understand (Mikkonen and Raphael 2010). To be historically displaced and treated as a second-class citizen (also referred to as "fourth-world status") in your own lands is one factor that must be considered. Another contributing factor that renders Indigenous peoples indiscernible – even invisible – is the categorization of 500 diverse Indigenous Nations under the umbrella of multiculturalism. Homogenizing educational practices continues to block Indigenous youth from fully participating in schools (Barman 2011).

So, what works? How can we facilitate Indigenous student success in high schools? Research into the factors that support Indigenous students are (Bell et al. 2004):

- inter-agency collaborations that focus on the whole student (physical, emotional, intellectual, and spiritual needs)
- Indigenous safe spaces in schools (designated room with an education counsellor, Elder/Métis Senator, and learning resources such as computers and printers)
- engagement with parents/guardians/communities (with clear plans and policies on how to meaningfully include these stakeholders)
- pedagogical and curriculum practices that are culturally relevant (strategies and content that honour Indigenous practices and traditions in secondary-school courses)
- transition programs with continuous follow up (e.g., elementary to secondary, secondary to postsecondary, mentorship, cooperative opportunities)
- retention/graduation plans that have alternate pathways (while a four-year high-school plan is typical, a five- or six-year plan could be considered, with options – such as alternative, online)
- educational spaces committed to equity and inclusion, and that celebrate diversity and heterogeneity
- professional learning communities in secondary schools where school boards set aside time and money to ensure teachers can attend training, and where in-services for teachers focus on action research and social-justice initiatives

Retention

For the purposes of this section, retention refers to those practices, programs, policies, and personnel that contribute to keeping Indigenous youth in school (Toulouse 2010). See figure 4.1 for a model:

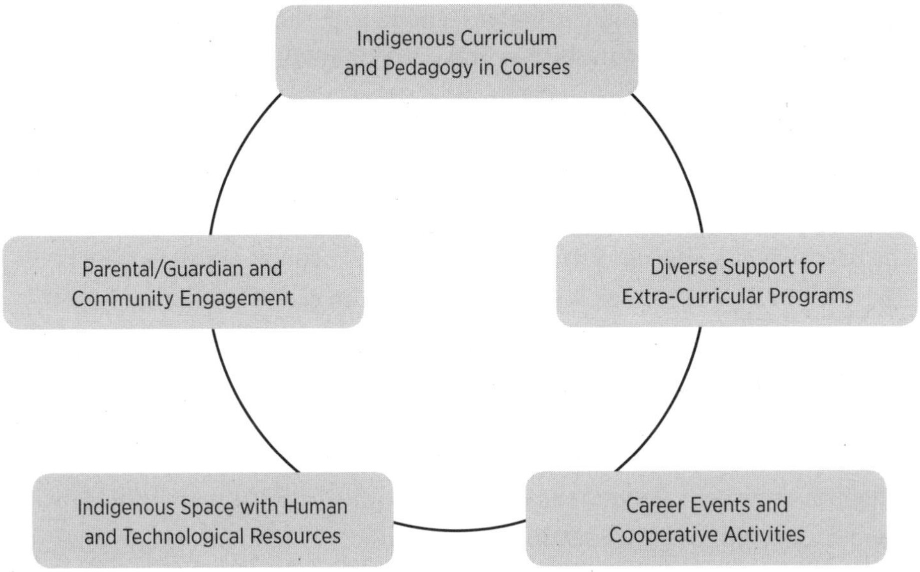

Figure 4.1. *Retention Considerations. This model focuses primarily on factors affecting retention. Consideration for all the needs of the Indigenous student is essential.*

Poverty is an issue many Indigenous students and their families face. It has been proven that low socioeconomic status places children and youth at risk for a variety of life-altering conditions. The social determinants of health are key to understanding why certain populations are thriving and others are not (Mikkonen and Raphael 2010). Indigenous communities living with financial challenges and intergenerational issues also face uncertain food and job security, inadequate housing, nonavailability of social safety nets, and inaccessibility to education.

These are real, everyday concerns many Indigenous students in high school face, in both urban and rural settings. This is why it is so important for educators to become advocates at a variety of levels for Indigenous learners and their families.

Indigenous youth who become involved in extra-curricular activities feel a sense of belonging to a caring community, and this is a major factor to their success in high school (Council of Ministers of Education, Canada 2010). However, extra-curricular activities like sports, clubs, events, and socials in secondary schools usually require equipment, fees, transportation, additional time, and potential materials. Knowing many Indigenous students face multiple challenges, schools and their teachers need to be aware of organizations in the community that can help. These resources – friendship centres, First Nation bands, Indigenous government agencies, Métis organizations, Inuit groups, Indigenous health access centres, and other social networks – can provide potential supports for those students who require them to fully participate in school activities. It is essential to learn about

Important Note!
Intergenerational issues can often refer to the effects of residential schooling and other forms of colonialism inflicted upon Indigenous peoples. These issues can often manifest in negative ways (e.g., higher rates of poverty, depression, substance abuse, lack of self-esteem, lower graduation rates).

students' personal and home situations, and to gain their trust. Many students may have additional responsibilities at home as caretakers for younger siblings or other family members. Social networks can provide important community connections to Indigenous youth, inviting them to participate in extra-curricular activities.

Designated spaces with human and material resources are also pivotal in the retention of Indigenous students in secondary schools (Donovan 2011). These culturally safe rooms are places where youth can access technology (e.g., computers, Internet, printers) and assistance (e.g., education counsellor, tutor) to complete assignments and investigate additional support (e.g., housing, employment, counselling). Cultural advisors such as Elders, Métis Senators, and other knowledge holders should also be included in the school environment. Events, workshops, and other activities can be held in these designated spaces (Assembly of First Nations 2012b). Below are some secondary schools, centres, communities, and programs that are models for supporting Indigenous learners:

- Lightning Trail Program with the District School Board Ontario North East and Northern College in Timmins, Ontario
- Nbisiing Secondary School in Nipissing First Nation, Ontario
- N'Swakamok Native Alternative School in Sudbury, Ontario
- Manitoba First Nations Education Resource Centre in Winnipeg, Manitoba
- Atikameg School in Whitefish Lake First Nation Reserve, Alberta
- Merritt Secondary School in Merritt, British Columbia

The above list is a starting point for researching wise practices to facilitate Indigenous student success in secondary school. It is not all encompassing.

Providing cooperative experiences and linking academic studies to a variety of real career options are instrumental to Indigenous students (Association of Universities and Colleges of Canada 2013). Attending fairs (real and online) that address postsecondary opportunities, potential business ventures, exchange programs, and job prospects are all important. Mentorship systems and interactions with role models also assist in facilitating success for Indigenous learners. Courses in high school that lead to a diploma must always have relevancy and clear multiple pathways (Richards 2013). The following are some of the Indigenous organizations that can provide career information:

- Canadian Council for Aboriginal Business in Toronto, Ontario
- Aboriginal Financial Officers Association in Ottawa, Ontario
- AboriginalCareers.ca in Winnipeg, Manitoba
- Indspire in Oshweken, Ontario

- Aboriginal Futures in Calgary, Alberta
- Aboriginal Human Resource Council in Saskatoon, Saskatchewan

While educators can use these resources, it is also important to begin with your local Indigenous agencies and supports.

Parental, guardian, and community engagement with schools is essential to Indigenous student success in secondary education. Nearly every school board entrusted with First Nations, Métis, and Inuit education has some sort of plan on how to meaningfully involve Indigenous peoples in schools. Youth need networks of both immediate and extended family to face their challenges, overcome obstacles, and celebrate their achievements (Hardes 2013). The connections to self-esteem, purpose, and culture are embedded in the implementation of these plans.

***ACHIEVING ABORIGINAL STUDENT SUCCESS* BY TOULOUSE**	***FNMI PRESENCE IN RAINBOW SCHOOLS* BY RDSB**
Establish a relationship with the Indigenous education counsellor or Indigenous lead to support students.	Provide translation services for school-to-home and home-to-school communication for Indigenous parents.
Ensure the foyer and entrance at your school have the Indigenous greetings of your population.	Plan orientation sessions for parents/guardians with transportation and child care arranged at site.
Hold a school welcoming feast at the school or at a neutral location for the students and their families.	Organize mobile and virtual parent and guardian centres with events, resources, and services.

Figure 4.2. *Community Engagement. This model represents select examples from the author and from the Rainbow District School Board (RDSB) of how to engage the Indigenous community. The foundations of engagement are trust, time, and reciprocity.*

Figure 4.2 provides a concise summary of unique strategies from two useful resources that respectfully address the preceding themes:

First, Indigenous curriculum and meaningful pedagogy underpin the connection Indigenous students have with high-school courses (Deer 2013a, b). Teaching and learning strategies must be differentiated and have real-life attachments and meanings. Infusing First Nations, Métis, and Inuit histories, contributions, world-view, and events throughout each subject is also critical (Gray and Partington 2012). Students need to see their communities are valued; this type of education (involving Indigenous partners) also provides non-Indigenous students a new lens to understand the First Peoples of Canada.

Second, learning resources that are authentic, challenge stereotypes, and promote respectful relationships are also needed in this approach. Some Indigenous publishers and centres where you can access such resources are:

- GoodMinds.com in Oshweken, Ontario
- Theytus Books in Penticton, British Columbia
- Pemmican Publications in Winnipeg, Manitoba
- Strong Nations in Nanaimo, British Columbia
- Inhabit Media Inc. in Iqaluit, Nunavut
- Oneida Language Centre in Southwold, Ontario
- HighWater Press in Winnipeg, Manitoba
- Portage and Main Press in Winnipeg, Manitoba

Also, investigate the materials purchased by your school board. Ensure these resources have been vetted through an Indigenous review process.

Transition

Transition refers to those practices, programs, policies, and personnel that contribute to the shifts from one educational stage to another (Toulouse 2010). I had the privilege of working with the Ontario Native Education Counselling Association (ONECA) on several research projects aimed at Indigenous student success. One of these projects, called "Transitions," is a leading program to facilitate school and life changes from one level to the next. Transitions is a multistage project that includes an interactive website (<www.oneca.com/transitions/>) for students, parents/guardians, education counsellors, other professionals, and community members. The website has a series of videos, downloadable brochures, and links that document how to assist Indigenous students with moving from the various levels in school and life (preschool to elementary, elementary to secondary, secondary to postsecondary, between institutions, postsecondary to work, and going home).

Elementary to Secondary

Moving from elementary school to secondary school is one of the most dramatic changes in any student's life – especially for Indigenous students. Developmentally, this age is one of the most challenging, as youth often feel misunderstood and rely heavily on peers for acceptance (Assembly of First Nations 2012a, b). Self-esteem is fragile, and students are the most impressionable during this stage. Fitting in and seeking meaning with friends are the priorities. This is the time when supports are the most needed. When our youth move from elementary school to high school, research suggests the following strategies be implemented (Council of Ministers of Education, Canada 2010):

- Site visits to the secondary school when other students are not present (i.e., during summer) to give Indigenous students the opportunity to locate the places they will be frequenting (e.g., homeroom, cafeteria, classrooms, gym, library, designated Native space). One of students' greatest fears is walking into the wrong classroom.
- Mentorship programs during the final years of elementary, in which secondary peers come to visit elementary students at their schools. These programs could consist of mini-workshops on how to be successful and how to have fun in high school (e.g., studying techniques, academic supports, clubs, events).
- Connecting parents/guardians with support networks and agencies that focus on children and youth (e.g., other parent groups, mental-health teams, recreation and leisure activities, libraries, food banks). Ensure transportation, child care, and translation services are available for parents/guardians.
- Key secondary personnel (e.g., principal, counsellors, teachers, mentors) attend an event – such as a grade-eight graduation ceremony, powwow, workshops – where the graduating elementary students and their families will be present. Secondary personnel need to interact with incoming students and their families. This sets the tone of a caring community.
- Welcoming feast for new students and their families before the school year begins. Arrange transportation and infuse local traditions as part of this event.

Secondary and Postsecondary

Moving from secondary to postsecondary (or to the world of work) is also a major transition in a student's life. The greatest challenges Indigenous students will face are financial and emotional. Although some First Nations and Inuit students are eligible for funding through their bands or organizations to attend college or university, the amount they receive is often well below the poverty line. When students leave family, friends, and a community they have resided in for a period of time, their social network is weakened by geography, new living arrangements, and new and emerging responsibilities (Hardes 2013). Figure 4.3 provides a brief summary of some strategies that can be implemented to assist Indigenous students with the transition.

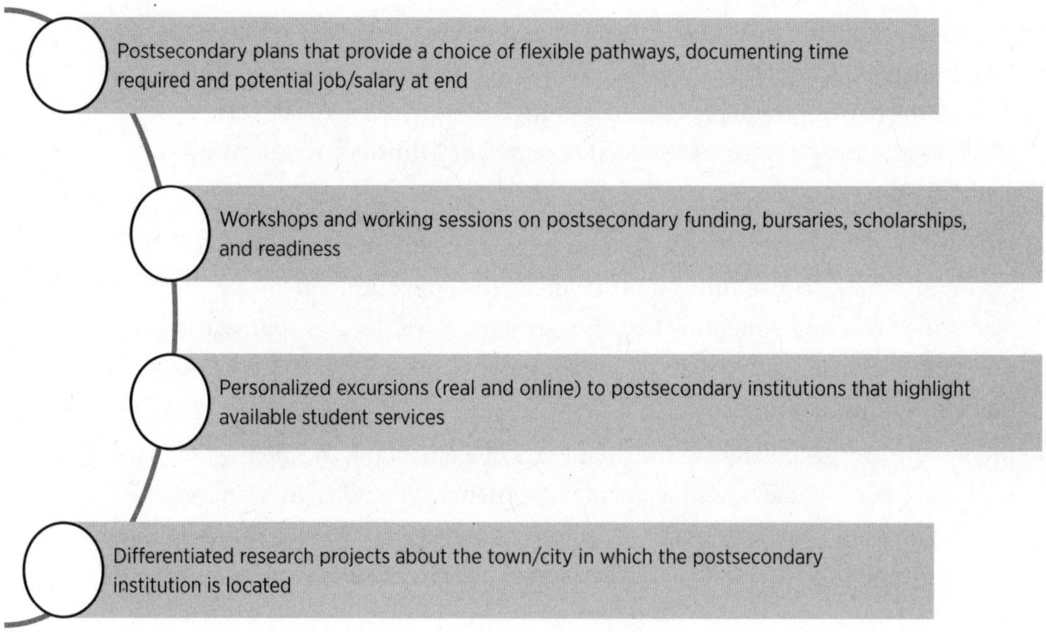

Figure 4.3. *Transition Strategies. This model provides a selection of strategies that address the transition from secondary school to postsecondary.*

Many Indigenous students may choose to enter the work force directly from high school. This transition requires an alternative plan to successfully assist youth with this change (Donovan 2011). Some suggested strategies are the following:

- cooperative education, internships, and job-shadowing programs in the final years of high school that may turn into an entry-level position or an opportunity to network for another role
- workshops with an Indigenous local delivery mechanism (e.g., Aboriginal Business Canada or a similar agency) to develop a small-business plan with loan applications
- mini-sessions throughout the year that contribute toward a guidance (career education) credit that focuses on resumes, interviewing, job searches, living skills, and other relevant topics
- youth conferences that provide information on exchanges and volunteering with other communities (local and global), emphasizing the benefits/challenges of these experiences

Graduation

Graduation is the culmination of all those practices, programs, policies, and personnel that lead to Indigenous students' attainment of the secondary-school diploma (Toulouse 2010). To honour the importance of this milestone, educators need to realize that each Indigenous student who graduates from high school comes from a community. In other words, each student's graduation affects a group of people made up of siblings, cousins, aunts, uncles, parents, grandparents, and other family members (some family members may not be blood related but are just as significant). The success of this singular student is an intergenerational one that potentially builds capacity in an Indigenous Nation (Chiefs Assembly on Education 2012). Building capacity in Indigenous communities refers to an overall effect where pride in individual and group accomplishments inspires change. These changes vary from community to community. However, higher self-esteem, understanding of colonialism, empowerment, increased graduation rates, increased health and wellness, increased businesses, and other socioeconomic improvements may be seen. Many of us do not understand the significance of Indigenous students who graduate from secondary school, and I highly encourage educators to attend a community-based celebration to understand the pride associated with this event.

Ensuring Indigenous students graduate from secondary school is the responsibility of all educators (Bell et al. 2004). It is also a gift knowing you have contributed to the life of an individual who will give back to his or her community. Indigenous students are often motivated to complete their schooling so they can make a difference to their families. Each graduate becomes a role model (whether aware of it or not) and an example of the resiliency of Indigenous youth.

The role of the secondary teacher in the graduation continuum is critical (Richards 2013). Educators have a significant impact on whether or not an Indigenous student completes his or her courses. Academic readiness, culturally relevant pedagogy, critical thinking, technology, building self-esteem, and reflection are taught by teachers committed to having Indigenous students graduate. So, what does this actually mean? Where do we begin in this commitment to inclusive practice?

First, consider the following facts as part of your own basic knowledge about Indigenous students and their families (Chiefs Assembly on Education 2012; Gray and Partington 2012):

- All lands in Canada were the traditional territories of Indigenous peoples.
- There are 14 treaties in Canada signed between Indigenous peoples and the Crown (prior to 1923). These treaties outline the inherent rights of the First Peoples of the land.
- These current treaties concern approximately 75 percent of the landmass in Canada.
- These treaties and the inherent rights of Indigenous peoples are further guaranteed and affirmed under Section 35 (1) of the *Constitution Act* (1982).

- The *Jay Treaty* of 1794 was signed by Great Britain and the United States. It stated Indigenous peoples in Canada were free to enter the United States for a variety of purposes (e.g., work, immigration, travel, school).
- There are 633 First Nation communities in Canada that belong to 11 distinct language families (with over 60 unique dialects).
- The Inuit are very diverse and are represented by a national organization that refers to their traditional lands in Nunatsiavut (Labrador), Nunavik (northern Quebec), Nunavut, and the Inuvialuit Settlement Region in the Northwest Territories.
- The Métis have distinct traditions, cultures, world-views, and histories. In 2006, 400 000 Canadians self-identified as Métis. Ninety percent (90%) of this population live in the western provinces.
- There are eight Métis settlements in northern Alberta, which includes 1.2 million acres of traditional lands.
- One in four Indigenous children lives in poverty. The rate is much higher in remote areas and lower in urban centres where Indigenous services are available.
- By 2026, Indigenous peoples are forecasted to make up 4.6 percent of the Canadian population.

Second, we can take this knowledge acquisition further by examining the concepts in figure 4.4 through the creation of a critical biography.

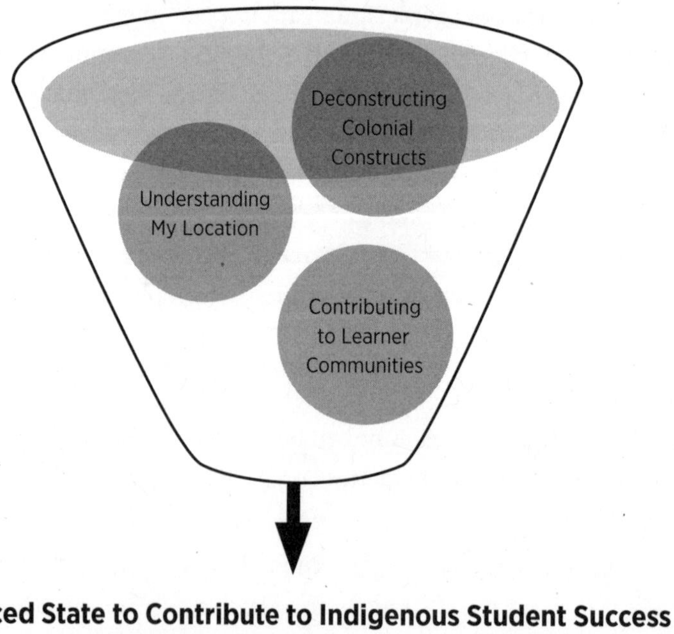

Figure 4.4. *Critical Concepts and Understandings. This model focuses on the concepts underlying the creation of a critical biography by the teacher and/or education professional. These are understandings the teacher and/or education professional engage in and then can add to their own professional portfolios as culturally competent practices.*

A Critical Biography for Teachers and Education Professionals

A critical biography is based on the research surrounding cultural competency and decolonization (Battiste 2013; Huber 2010). It provides educators with a different lens to view the self and reflect on the realities that face their Indigenous students (and other potentially marginalized groups or students at risk). The creation of this biography should take the form and represent the particular learning styles of the educator(s) (e.g., collage, journal, research paper, poster presentation, song, video, photo montage). It is suggested that the critical biography be done as part of a Professional Learning Community (PLC) or as part of a school and/or board-wide professional development initiative (ongoing or focused sessions). This supports the importance and legitimacy of the biography and its application to the classroom setting and student success plans.

The content of the critical biography is based on information shared through mini-lessons and discussions between teachers and education professionals. These critical conversations emerge from the elements illustrated in figure 4.4 (see page 54) and as further described here:

- **Understanding my location** involves identifying how our lives are embedded with power, privilege, and challenge (Deer 2013b). As an example, if we go back to the social determinants of health, Indigenous status predisposes this group to a series of inequitable conditions (e.g., poverty, lack of job security). A critical biography of who we are provides insight into our strengths and biases. It can become the catalyst for change, because it serves many functions. One is it gives a picture of the self, our environments, and the forces that have shaped us. Another is it provides us with insight into the advantages and disadvantages we may have by virtue of race, religion, culture, gender, educational level, marital status, economic status, postal code, and so on. A critical biography provides a lens for reframing and understanding why we think the way we do, feel the way we do, and act the way we do. This is absolutely essential for developing a reflective stance that enables one to relate to others. We can never truly understand the experiences of others (e.g., Indigenous peoples who have been the focus of cultural genocide), but we can create safe intersections for talking and relating (Friesen and Krauth 2012). For example, sharing incidents/events like having a rental application immediately turned down because your name is First Nations or having a classroom of students interrogate an Indigenous student when a blockade or social-justice movement regarding Indigenous peoples is localized is a starting point. It is important for teachers to try to imagine what this would be like – to be targeted (and humiliated) because of race and ignorance.

To transform the preceding description into real terms for teachers and education professionals, the following elements should be discussed in this section of the critical biography:

- name
- culture
- language(s)
- gender
- social class
- marital status
- family status
- sexual orientation
- religion
- education level
- socioeconomic status
- occupation(s)
- geographical location (origin and current)
- other (deemed as necessary)

After this phase has been completed, the next stage is to identify the core values inherited as a result of these factors (positive, negative, neutral, do not know). If we are unsure of what a certain factor may represent, we may have to ask for a colleague's opinion. This then becomes the space to look at how our lives have certain strengths and certain challenges. A final aspect of this process is to share with others in a community of diversity, objectivity, and respect (Lamb 2014). This can be done in a small-group setting with an experienced facilitator (e.g., guidance counsellor, Elder) or privately with a colleague or mentor we trust.

As a teacher in secondary school, this critical biography helps us frame the way we approach Indigenous students. If we know this student has financial barriers or lives with extended family or has parents/guardians whose first language is not English, our support, consideration, and search for appropriate resources change (Gray and Partington 2012). This process can result in reflective action where patience and responsiveness reside.

- **Deconstructing colonial constructs** means we acknowledge that everyone has been affected by colonialism (Barman 2011). All peoples have been colonized to some degree (e.g., as part of socialization, pop culture, education). The recognition and acceptance of this leads us toward a path for breaking down any embedded biases and challenging them head on. All peoples (Indigenous and non-Indigenous) need to begin with the understanding that we all share the experiences of grief, pain, anger, shame, happiness, joy, enlightenment, pride, and so on. No one group has the monopoly on emotions. What differs is the breadth of these experiences and the structural, societal, and historical barriers that may have led to them. I have been in too many sessions where different groups try to privilege their pain from the others. Such people discount the feelings of others and assume their pain is more important than anyone else's. This type of approach does not lead to building relationships or facilitating change. It creates an atmosphere of blame, apathy, and fear.

Deconstructing colonial constructs concerns itself with truth-telling exercises (Deer 2013b). These range from reading articles about the impacts of sports logos (that have Indigenous stereotypes) on the self-esteem of Indigenous peoples and how this can desensitize others from seeing Indigenous peoples as human beings; to learning the real facts about Indigenous Nations (e.g., the myth that Indigenous peoples get everything for free); to many other knowledge-lifting opportunities that challenge us to question, examine, and reexamine. In a secondary-school setting, this approach provides us with a chance to rethink our courses in terms of the resources, language, and pedagogy we use (Association of Universities and Colleges of Canada 2013).

- **Contributing to learner communities** involves engaging in professional activities that improve our practice as teachers (Bell et al. 2004). It means we first acknowledge all the things we do to promote student success. It also means we look at the practices in our classrooms that relate to student achievement and student well-being.

In conclusion, the critical biography can become the platform for further research on instructional and curricular change. Professional Learning Communities (PLCs), Inquiry Projects, Inter-Agency Collaborations, and the many other names this type of research goes by are critical to a teaching profession focused on equity. Indigenous students are counting on us to ensure we have the knowledge, tools, and critical sense of self to move forward together in classrooms fostered by inclusive educators.

Chapter 5.

INDIGENOUS THEMES AND MATERIAL RESOURCES

Many educators cite the lack of access to Indigenous resources as one of the major reasons they do not infuse Indigenous content into their courses (Goulet and McLeod 2013; Kumar 2011). Most school boards in Canada now have an Indigenous lead (or an appointed consultant) entrusted with providing resources and professional development. However, if your school does not have a lead, I have compiled a list of Indigenous-based books you will find useful. These books are organized by typical secondary-school subjects and have been vetted through an Indigenous review process. Many of these books (hard copy and electronic) are cross-curricular (used in science, but, also, have applications in other subjects). A prime example of a multi-curricular document is the series American Indian Contributions to the World by Keoke and Porterfield, which crosses all high-school subject areas.

The selection of texts that follows can be adapted for students in grades 9 to 12. The content can also be modified to suit the expectations/learning outcomes in a secondary-school teacher's respective courses.

English

Adventures of Rabbit and Bear Paws by Chad Solomon, ill. Christopher Solomon (2006; 2009; 2010; 2011)

As Long as the Rivers Flow: A Last Summer Before Residential School by Constance Brissenden and Larry Oskiniko Loyie, ill. Heather Holmand (2005)

Bearwalker by Joseph Bruchac (2007)

Bird Springs by Carolyn Marsden (2007)

A Blanket of Butterflies by Richard Van Camp, ill. Scott B. Henderson (2015)

Blood Red Ochre by Kevin Major (1996)

Buffy Sainte-Marie: It's My Way by Blair Stonechild (2012)

Country of Wolves: A Graphic Novel by Neil Christopher (2013)

The Dark Pond by Joseph Bruchac (2001)

Dog Tracks: A Novel by Ruby Slipperjack (2008)

Dream Catchers: Legend, Lore and Artifacts by Cath Oberholtzer (2012)

Edward Curtis Project: A Modern Picture Story by Marie Clements and Rita Leistner (2010)

Everything You Wanted to Know About Indians but Were Afraid to Ask by Anton Treuer (2012)

Face Pullers: Photographing Native Canadians 1871–1939 by Brock Silversides (1994)

Fatty Legs: A True Story by Christy Jordan-Fenton and Margaret Pokiak-Fenton (2010)

The 500 Years of Resistance Comic Book by Gord Hill (2010)

The Gift Is in the Making: Anishinaabeg Stories by Leanne Simpson (2013)

Healing Through Art by Zoey Wood-Salomon (2006)

The Heart of a Chief by Joseph Bruchac (2001)

Him Standing by Richard Wagamese (2013)

Hook Up by Kim Firmston (2012)

If I Ever Get Out of Here by Eric Gansworth (2013)

Indian Horse by Richard Wagamese (2012)

Killer of Enemies by Joseph Bruchac (2013)

The Lightning Strikes: A Novel of an All-Star American Indian Softball Team by Devon Mihesuah (2004)

The Loner by Dana Coates (2012)

Meet a Journalist: Waubgeshig Rice by Kim Ziervogel (2009)

The Middle of Everywhere by Monique Polak (2009)

Middle Row by Sylvia Olsen (2008)

The Night Wanderer: A Graphic Novel by Drew Hayden Taylor and Alison Kooistra, ill. Mike Wyatt (2013)

Night Wings by Joseph Bruchac (2009)

Nobody Cries at Bingo by Dawn Dumont (2011)

The Porcupine Year by Louise Erdrich (2008)

Rain Is Not My Indian Name by Cynthia Leitich Smith (2001)

Raven Brings the Light by Roy Henry Vickers, ill. Robert Budd (2013)

Red: A Haida Manga by Michael Nicoll Yahgulanaas (2011)

The Saver by Edeet Ravel (2008)

7 Generations: A Plains Cree Saga by David A. Robertson, ill. Scott B. Henderson (2012)

Sister to the Wolf by Maxine Trottier (2004)

The Star-Man and Other Tales by Basil Johnston and Jonas George (1997)

Story Keepers: Conversations with Aboriginal Writers by Jennifer David (2004)

Stray Dog Moccasins by Marilyn Dumont (2009)

Strength and Struggle: Perspectives from First Nations, Inuit and Métis Peoples in Canada by Rachel Mishenene and Pamela Rose Toulouse (2011)

Sugar Falls: A Residential School Story by David A. Robertson, ill. Scott B. Henderson (2012)
Sweetgrass Basket by Marlene Carvell (2005)
Thunderbird Spirit by Sigmund Brouwer (2008)
Trickster: Native American Tales, A Graphic Collection by Matt Dembicki (2010)
Truth and Bright Water by Thomas King (2001)
The Way by Joseph Bruchac (2007)
Whisper in the Dark by Joseph Bruchac (2009)
Winners by Mary-Ellen Lang Collura (1986)

Math

American Indian Contributions to the World: Science and Technology by Emory Dean Keoke and Kay Marie Porterfield (2005)
Beaded Earrings: Techniques and Designs by Rex Reddick and Ginger Reddick (2011)
Beadwork: First Peoples' Beading History and Techniques by Christi Belcourt (2010)
Blackfoot War Art: Pictographs of the Reservation Period, 1880–2000 by James Dempsey (2007)
Cross Stitch Patterns Based on Pacific Northwest Coast Native Indian Art Styles: Book 1 Thunderbirds by Jim Gilbert (2005)
Encyclopedia of American Indian Contributions to the World: 15 000 Years of Inventions and Innovations by Emory Dean Keoke and Kay Marie Porterfield (2003)
Floral Journey: Native North American Beadwork by Lois Sherr Dubin (2014)
A Manual of Fingerweaving by Robert Austin (2000)
Native American Mathematics by Michael Closs (1996)
Rainbow Crow Nagweyaabi-Aandeg by David Bouchard (2012)
Teaching Mathematics in a First Peoples Context by FNESC (2011)

Science

American Indian Contributions to the World: Buildings, Clothing and Art by Emory Dean Keoke and Kay Marie Porterfield (2005)
American Indian Contributions to the World: Medicine and Health by Emory Dean Keoke and Kay Marie Porterfield (2005)
American Indian Contributions to the World: Science and Technology by Emory Dean Keoke and Kay Marie Porterfield (2005)

Creations from the Heart: Native Crafts and Learning Activities by Jameson C. Brant (2006)

Do All Indians Live in Tipis? Questions and Answers from the National Museum of the American Indian by NMAI (2007)

The Drum Calls Softly by David Bouchard and Shelley Willier (2008)

Faces in the Forest: First Nations Art Created on Living Trees by Michael Blackstock (2001)

Flight of the Hummingbird: A Parable for the Environment by Michael Nicoll Yahgulanaas (2008)

Indian Givers: How Native Americans Transformed the World by Jack Weatherford (2010)

The Inuit Thought of It: Amazing Arctic Innovations by Alooktook Ipellie and David MacDonald (2007)

Moon Speaks Cree: A Winter Adventure by Larry Loyie and Constance Brissenden, ill. Bill Cohen (2013)

Our Knowledge Canoe by Marcel Labelle (2011)

Strength of the Earth: The Classic Guide to Ojibwe Uses of Native Plants by Frances Densmore and Brenda J. Child (2006)

Talking Rocks: Geology and 10,000 Years of Native American Tradition in the Lake Superior Region by Ron Morton and Carl Gawboy (2003)

Under the Ice by Rachel Qitsualik, ill. Jae Korim (2011)

History

Aboriginal Beliefs, Values, and Aspirations in Contemporary Society by Barbara Filion, Neal McLeod, and Shay-Lea O'Brien (2011)

Aboriginal Peoples: Building for the Future by Kevin Reed (1999)

Aboriginal Peoples in Canada by Kevin Reed, Mary Joy Elijah, and Keith Lickers (2011)

America's Gift: What the World Owes to the Americas and Their First Inhabitants by Kathe Roth and Denis Vaugeois (2009)

Betty: The Life of Helen Betty Osborne by David Alexander Robertson, ill. Scott B. Henderson (2015)

Chippewa Customs by Frances Densmore (1979)

Dakota Women's Work: Creativity, Culture, and Exile by Colette A. Hyman (2012)

Hidden in Plain Sight: Contributions of Aboriginal Peoples to Canadian Identity and Culture by David Newhouse, Cora Voyageur and Dan Beavon (v1:2005; v2:2011)

The Illustrated History of the Chippewas of Nawash by Polly Keeshig-Tobias (1996)

Louis Riel: A Comic-Strip Biography by Chester Brown (2006)

Mi'kmaq: Canadian Aboriginal Art and Culture by Christine Webster (2007)

Moccasin Creek by Rene Andre Meshake (2009)

Native Universe: Voices of Indian America by Native American Tribal Leaders, Writers, Scholars, and Storytellers by Gerald McMaster and Clifford Trafzer (2008)

Pīsim Finds Her Miskanow by William Dumas (2013)

Real Justice: Convicted for Being Mi'kmaq, The Story of Donald Marshall, Jr. by Bill Swan (2013)

The Secret of Your Name: Proud to be Métis by David Bouchard, music by John Arcand, ill. Denis Weber (2010)

Sugar Falls: A Residential School Story by David A. Robertson, ill. Scott B. Henderson (2011)

Warriors: Navajo Code Talkers by Kenji Kawano (1991)

The Winter People by Joseph Bruchac (2004)

Geography

American Indian Contributions to the World: Trade, Transportation and Warfare by Emory Dean Keoke and Kay Marie Porterfield (2005)

American Indian Places: A Historical Guide Book by Frances H. Kennedy (2008)

Kokum's Gift: Teachings from Ojibway and Cree Spirituality, Culture, and Traditions by Gordon Miller (2009)

Learning by Doing: Northwest Coast Native Indian Art by Karin Clark and Jim Gilbert (2000)

Living Our Cultures, Sharing Our Heritage: The First Peoples of Alaska by Aron A. Crowell, Rosita Worl, Paul Ongtooguk, and Dawn D. Biddison (2010)

Mikinak, Teacher Awareness Guide by the First Nations Education Council (n.d.)

Native American Arts and Cultures by Anne D'alleva (1993)

A Native American Thought of It: Amazing Inventions and Innovations by Rocky Landon and David Macdonald (2008)

No Borders: Kigliqangittuq by Darla Evyagotailak and Mindy Willett (2013)

Picture Rocks: American Indian Rock Art in the Northeast Woodlands by Edward Lenik (2002)

Salish: Canadian Aboriginal Art and Culture by Christine Webster (2008)

Health and Physical Education

American Indian Contributions to the World: Food, Farming and Hunting by Emory Dean Keoke and Kay Marie Porterfield (2005)

Arctic Thunder by Robert Feagan (2010)

Eating Well with Canada's Food Guide: First Nations, Inuit and Métis by Health Canada (2007)

Games of Survival: Traditional Inuit Games for Elementary Students by Johnny Issaluk (2013)

Looks Like Daylight: Voices of Indigenous Kids by Deborah Ellis (2013)

My Heroes Have Always Been Indians by Cora Voyageur (2010)

Native American Games and Stories by James Bruchac and Joseph Bruchac (2000)

Native American Gardening: Stories, Projects and Recipes for Families by Michael J. Caduto and Joseph Bruchac (1996)

Native Athletes in Action by Vincent Shilling (2007)

Our Original Games: A Look at Aboriginal Sport in Canada by Bruce Miller (2008)

They Call Me Chief: Warriors on Ice by Don Marks (2008)

Three Feathers by Richard Van Camp (2015)

Where the Rivers Meet by Don Sawyer (2015)

White Girl by Sylvia Olsen (2005)

Integrated Arts (Music, Drama, Visual Arts)

Ancestral Portraits: The Colour of My People by Frederick R. McDonald (2002)

Andrew Qappik: Pangnirtung Memories by Darlene Coward Wight (2010)

Anishinaabeg Stories: Featuring Petroglyphs, Petrographs, and Wampum Belts by Lynn Gehl (2013)

Art from Fort Marion: The Silberman Collection by Joyce M. Szabo (2009)

Art of the Northwest Coast by Aldona Jonaitis (2006)

Before and After the Horizon: Anishinaabe Artists of the Great Lakes by David Penney and Gerald McMaster (2013)

Born of Clay: Ceramics from the National Museum of the American Indian by Ramiro Matos, Ann McMullen, and Felipe Solis (2005)

Canadian Aboriginal Biographies: Artists by Jennifer Howse (2013)

Canadian Aboriginal Biographies: Musicians by Kaite Goldsworthy (2013)

Encyclopedia of Native Music: More Than a Century of Recordings from Wax Cylinders to the Internet by Brian Wright-McLeod (2005)

First Nations Art Projects and Activities by Butch Dick and Karin Clark (1999)
Haudenoshone: Thanksgiving Arts and Crafts by Jameson C. Brant (2012)
Meet a Music Industry Professional: Alan Greyeyes by Kim Ziervogel (2009)
Native Musicians in the Groove by Vincent Schilling (2009)
Only Drunks and Children Tell the Truth by Drew Hayden Taylor (1998)
This Path We Travel: Celebrations of Contemporary Native American Creativity by Charlotte Heth (1994)

Professional Development

Achieving Aboriginal Student Success: A Guide for K to 8 Classrooms by Pamela Rose Toulouse (2011)
Kinamagawin: Aboriginal Issues in the Classroom by the Centre for Aboriginal Culture and Education at Carleton University (2011)
Teaching Virtues: Building Character Across the Curriculum by Don Trent Jacobs and Jessica Jacobs-Spencer (2001)

Connections to Indigenous Lifelong Learning Concepts

After selecting a material resource (e.g., *A Blanket of Butterflies* by Richard Van Camp) for use in a secondary course (e.g., English), identify the themes (i.e., the grace of family AND trusting the power of the spirit world) in the material resource that complement the provincial/territorial curriculum (e.g., Ontario – English, Grade 9, Academic – Oral Communication – Demonstrating Understanding of Content), as well as the lifelong learning concepts valued by First Nations (*There are various sources of knowledge – seen and unseen*), Métis (*Sources of knowledge and knowing are diverse*), and Inuit (*Informal and formal learning are valued*) (Friesen and Ezeife 2013).

The contents in figures 5.1, 5.2, and 5.3 have been adapted from the holistic lifelong learning models developed by Indigenous communities and recorded by the Canadian Council on Learning (2007). The two questions that guide an educator's review of these models are:

1. Can I find the Indigenous concepts (or key words/phrases) that reflect themes from my selected material resource?
2. Can I match these themes to the outcomes/expectations in my secondary course and/or curriculum?

The responses to these questions can become that respectful link to Indigenous educational world-view/perspectives for yourself, your students, and connections to course content.

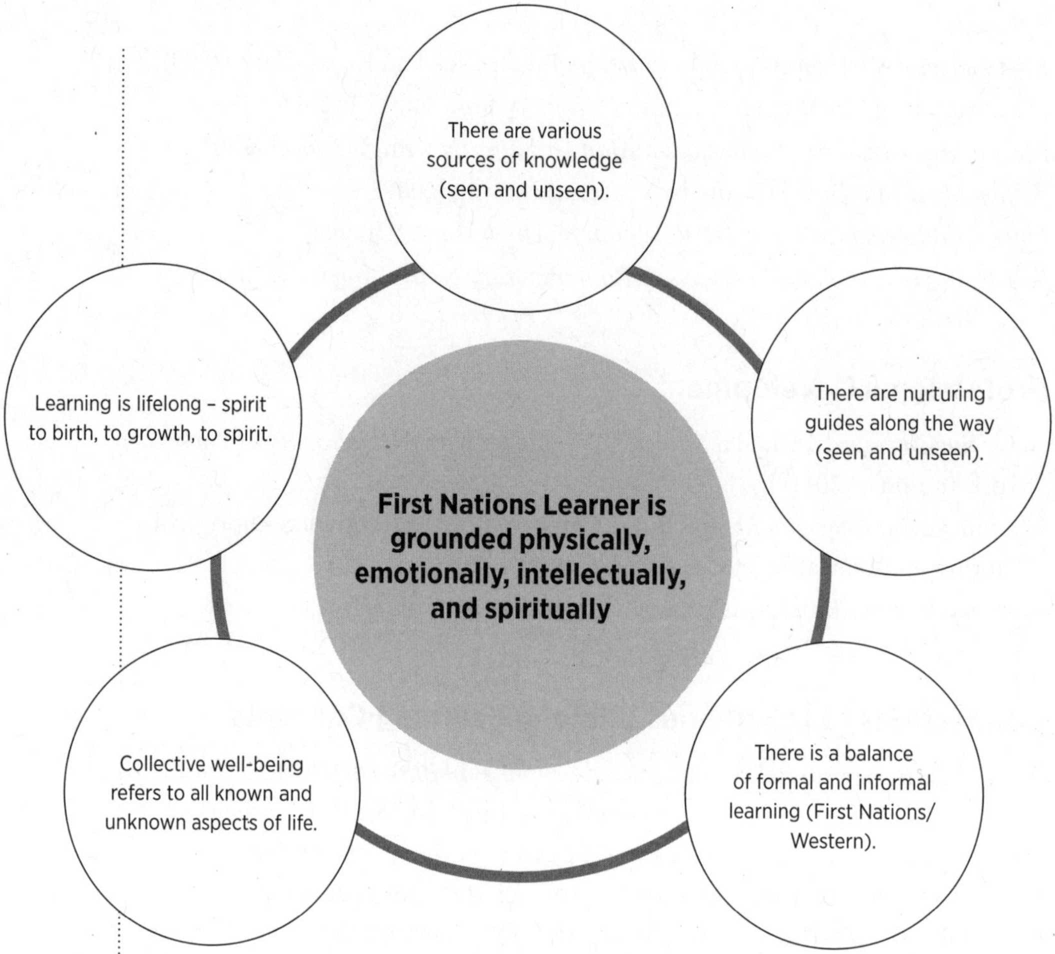

Figure 5.1. *First Nations Model. This model emerged from the First Nations group entrusted with developing a balanced First Nations perspective on lifelong learning. The concepts are based in the physical, emotional, intellectual, and spiritual aspects of self. Surrounding this central idea are the values of formal and informal education and recognition of seen/unseen teachers.*

Key words and phrases associated with this First Nations model are :

languages
traditions
ceremonies
ancestors
family
self
community
clan
Nation
Elders
Mother Earth
sacred
interconnectedness
intergenerational learning
workplace learning
mystery
stewardship
Creator
sacredness
all is living
elements – fire, earth, air, water
opportunities for learning, life, and career
metaphor of tree of life, with rings representing ongoing learning
—(Canadian Council on Learning 2007)

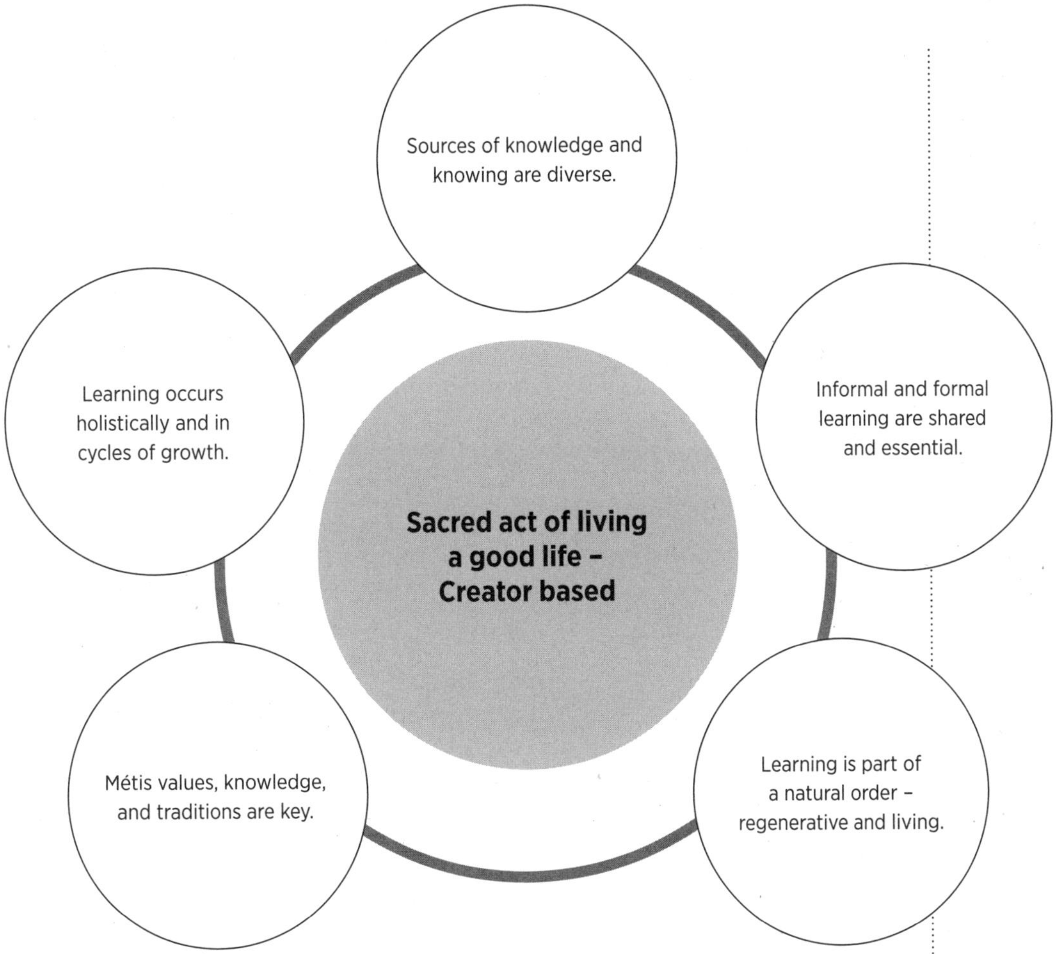

Figure 5.2. *Métis Model. This model emerged from the Métis group entrusted with developing a balanced Métis perspective on lifelong learning. The concepts represent the central idea of living a good life with the Creator. Surrounding this model are Métis traditions and an honouring of learning as a cycle.*

Key words and phrases associated with this Métis model are:

self
people
land
imagination
family
Métis Senators
traditional practices
medicines
herbs
language (i.e., Michif)
thinking
creativity
spiritual
physical
mental
emotional
access to opportunities
engagement of family in learning
various environments of growth (e.g., social, economic, political)
balance and harmony
giving back and contributing
metaphor of tree with roots, leaves, air, and connections to life
—(Canadian Council on Learning 2007)

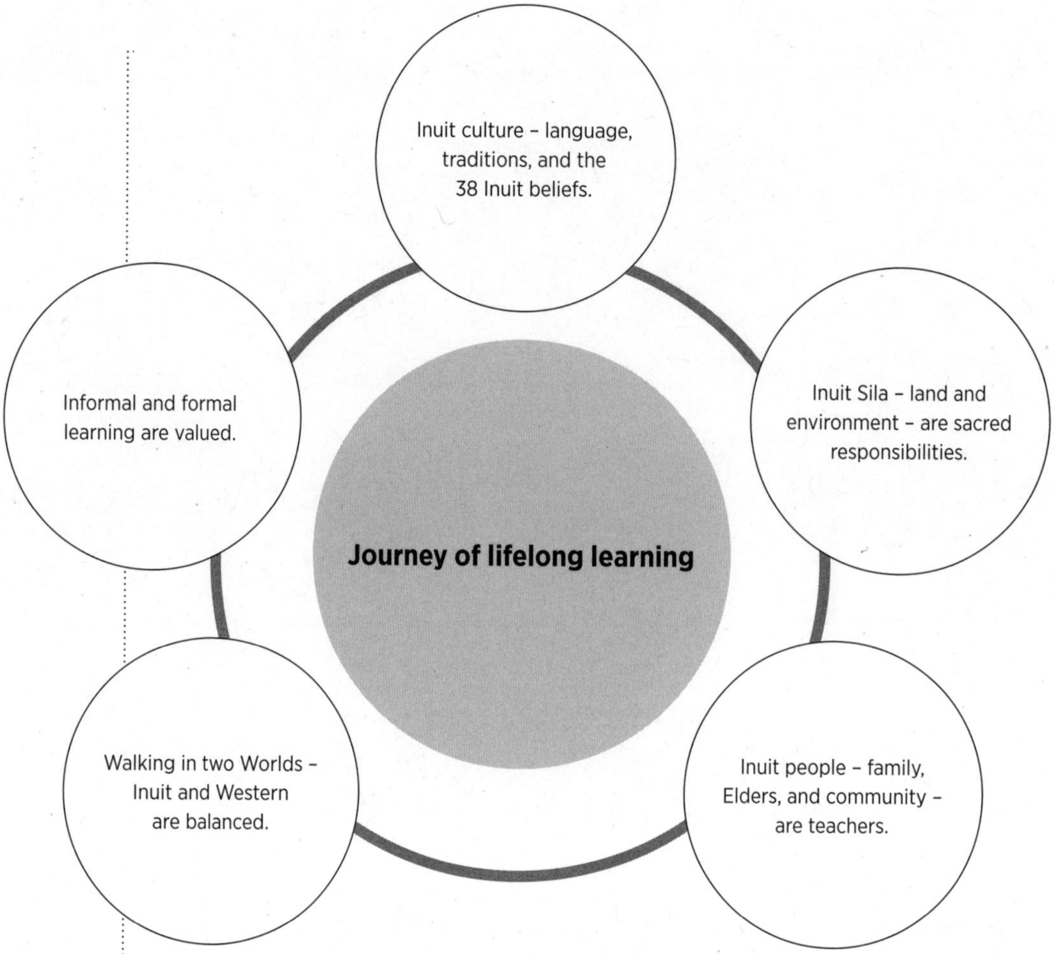

Figure 5.3. *Inuit Model. This model emerged from the Inuit group entrusted with developing a balanced Inuit perspective on lifelong learning. The concepts are grounded in knowledge acquisition as a living journey. Surrounding this model are the importance of land (sacred responsibility) and Inuit people as core teachers.*

Key words and phrases associated with this Inuit model are:

well-being is environmental, social, physical, economic, and community enriched
resilience
consensus
endurance
strength
generosity
respect
unity
apologize
acceptance
trust
helping
equality
improvisation
taking the long view
conservation
teamwork
moving forward
listening
adaptability
significance
observation
volunteer
unpretentious
mastery
oneness
metaphor of people holding a teaching blanket
—(Canadian Council on Learning 2007)

After identifying the Indigenous concepts and/or keywords/phrases (i.e., First Nations: *There are various sources of knowledge – seen and unseen;* Métis: *Sources of knowledge and knowing are diverse;* Inuit: *Informal and formal learning are valued*) in the material resource (e.g., *A Blanket of Butterflies* by Richard Van Camp), the next step is to complete a culturally appropriate lesson plan, using the format as described and included in this book (see Part 2). The final undertaking is to deliver the lesson, evaluate the effectiveness of the documents/strategies, and contribute to the co-generation of effective teaching practice by sharing these resources and ideas. As mentioned, it is always essential that educators draw upon local Indigenous resources first (e.g., human, material, geographical, events) to make the learning experiences more authentic. It is then important to offer secondary-school students a provincial, national, and international perspective to relate to Indigenous peoples (Anuik 2014). These efforts are key to building relationships and facilitating communities committed to each other. The benefits of including Indigenous materials and world-view are far-reaching. Educators who do so are clearly committed to social justice and change.

PART 2

CULTURALLY APPROPRIATE SECONDARY LESSONS BY GENERAL SUBJECT

INTRODUCTION TO PART 2: HOLISTIC LESSON FORMAT

The lessons that follow take an holistic approach modelled on Indigenous pedagogy and student success. To ensure a balanced consideration of student learning takes place, each lesson focuses on all four aspects of the Ojibwe living wheel: spiritual, physical, emotional, and intellectual.

The background information has the prerequisite knowledge (including key terms) each educator needs to move forward with each lesson. Teachers should review the background information first.

The **Spiritual** represents an Indigenous concept, a specific teaching, an historical fact, or a traditional use, and is shared with the students. Enlarge, display, and/or share the chosen teaching or fact during the Minds-On portion of the lesson so that all students can refer to it throughout the classroom activities. It is critical to continually make connections back to the spiritual.

The **Physical** represents the time, materials, resources, considerations, and suggested adaptations by grade required to implement (or further enhance) the lesson with the whole class. It is important to know that each of these lessons is an introductory knowledge springboard about the topic. These lessons are to be delivered first if students have not had this content. If your students have had experience with the topic, then focus the lesson further with the Suggested Adaptations by Grade.

The **Emotional** represents the strategies required for student engagement and includes the learning goal and step-by-step plans to carry out the lesson with the students. It is critical that the teacher review this section thoroughly to map out or adjust the lesson plan. The learning goal is the desired expectation/outcome of the lesson. This goal is supported through the hands-on classroom activities. It begins with a Minds-On activity that is essential for focusing the learning and creating curiosity about the topic. It ends with a Consolidation activity that connects the learning to the students' experiences and personalizes it to their world-view.

The **Intellectual** represents the assessment strategies and reproducible masters (RM) necessary to carry out and/or further develop the lesson with the class. The reproducibles consist of the various information sheets and organizers required for the lesson.

1.0 ENGLISH LESSON PLAN

Background Information for Teachers

In Indigenous societies, trickster stories exist as a means to teach about behaviour. The tales of hi-jinx and craftiness of tricksters serve as discussion points about social norms and mores. Life lessons and creative ways to understand how things came to be in our world also serve a function in trickster lore. There are many types of tricksters; some of the more familiar characters are:

Waynaboozhoo

Raven

Coyote

Glooscap

Key Terms

trickster: being in traditional Indigenous stories that helps to reinforce respectful behaviour through its own tales of hi-jinx

norm: belief or set of beliefs that a group identifies as acceptable behaviour amongst its members

Spiritual

The trickster comes by many names and forms in the 500 Nations. It may be a coyote, raven, raccoon, rabbit, elemental being like the wind/thunder, or spirit. However, two common characteristics of all tricksters are craftiness and the ability to disrupt the order of things in life. Tricksters are teachers to us all. We learn from their tales of mischief, and nearly every Indigenous Nation has a trickster in its traditional stories.

Physical

Time: 75 minutes

Materials/Resources

- Literature Circle Role Cards (RM 1.1)
- scissors
- *Trickster: Native American Tales: A Graphic Collection* by Dembicki (2010), or go to: <www.native-languages.org/trickster.htm> or <www.warpaths2peacepipes.com/native-american-culture/trickster.htm>
- computer/tablet with Internet access (optional)
- projector
- pens and pencils
- sticky notes
- masking tape
- variety of paper
- pencil crayons (variety of colours)

Considerations

- Locate a local Indigenous name and image for the trickster. Share with the students.
- Do not oversimplify the role and impact the trickster has on Indigenous cultures in terms of teachings and values.

Suggested Adaptations by Grade

9 – Select details from one of the stories or resources, and create a trickster profile. Relate this to personal experiences or pop culture today.
10 – Create a Venn diagram that documents the differences and similarities between one of the tricksters and another character.
11 – Identify the norms and mores presented in the story or resources. Locate articles (paper and online) that highlight the relevance of these teachings.
12 – Analyze the text features of one of these stories or resources (e.g., colours, fonts, layouts, language). Determine how altering a particular text feature can affect the story or resource.

Emotional

Learning Goal

To appreciate trickster stories and see their relevance in our contemporary world.

Step by Step

Minds-On

1. Give each student a sticky note. Have students record (in a manner they choose) their understanding of the word *trickster.*
2. Have each student post his or her sticky note (as an entry ticket) on a classroom wall. As a class, review each student's interpretation.

During

1. Select one of the stories from the Dembicki book or one of the suggested websites (see Materials/Resources, page 76) for the content of your lesson.
2. Using a projector, present a passage from the book or website. Share with the class.
3. Distribute a variety of paper and pencil crayons to each student. Offering a choice in paper (colours and sizes) contributes to differentiated strategies in the classroom. Students will use these materials to complete the tasks described on the role cards.
4. Photocopy Literature Circle Role Cards (RM 1.1), and cut out the cards. Give each student a card. As a class, review the six different roles and tasks. Tell students they are to follow the instructions on their role card during the next sharing of the text passage from the book or website. Reinforce there is no right way or wrong way for them to record their responses.
5. Do a second sharing of the passage. Give students about five minutes to complete their individual literature circle role tasks.
6. Organize students into same-role groups. In their groups, have each student take one to two minutes to share what he or she learned from the passage.
7. Organize students into different-role groups (1 through 6). Each student has one to two minutes to share what he or she learned individually and from others in the same-role group.
8. Have students post their work on a wall.
9. Invite students to share with the class what they have learned and how these teachings may or may not relate to their own lives.

Important Note! Share the spiritual insight and the key terms as a point of reference throughout this lesson for yourself and the students.

Consolidation

Select one of the questions below to synthesize and contemporize the learning from the lesson.

- What questions would you ask the trickster?
- Do you think the trickster is a positive or a negative force? Why?
- What is your opinion of a selected trickster? Provide evidence.
- How would you portray a trickster in a contemporary story?

Intellectual

Assessment

For – Entry tickets on their prior knowledge of the term *trickster.*

As – Peers sharing their information based on roles, beginning in groups of same roles and then moving back to a home group (diverse roles).

Of – Responses to a select question that consolidates the understanding of the trickster.

Extensions

- Complete a similar activity with one of the other graphic stories in *Trickster* or another resource.
- Invite a local Indigenous storyteller to the classroom to tell trickster stories.

Literature Circle Role Cards

1 Summarizer: Your role is to carefully listen to and view the passage. At the same time, you will record the four key points that outline the passage from beginning to end.

2 Visualizer: Your role is to carefully listen to and view the passage. At the same time, you will draw a picture that captures what you are hearing and seeing.

3 Questioner: Your role is to carefully listen to and view the passage. At the same time, you will record four questions that stem from this passage.

4 Webber: Your role is to carefully listen to and view the passage. At the same time, you will develop a web with four to six ideas, thoughts, and/or words related to it.

5 Wordsmith: Your role is to carefully listen to and view the passage. At the same time, you will record four words from the passage that are new, interesting, or require more explanation.

6 Meaning Maker: Your role is to carefully listen to and view the passage. At the same time, you will record two points telling how this tale relates to your own life or to the life of someone you know.

2.0 MATH LESSON PLAN

Background Information for Teachers

Beads were traditionally made from shells, animal bones, horns, teeth, stones, wood, and precious metals. They were carved or smelted into shapes by Indigenous craftspersons. Glass beads (various colours and sizes) were not introduced in North America until colonial traders began settlement. These multicoloured and multisized beads have now become the preferred material of Indigenous crafters. Each Indigenous Nation is known for a particular style of beading and functional item (i.e., clothing, bags, moccasins, mukluks, other). The beading designs and functional items often represent the lands from which the beadworkers originate. For example, the Ojibwe are known for their flower designs and bandolier bags. These designs represent the flora of Ojibwe lands, and the bag carried medicines of the Midewin people (spiritual society of the Anishinaabe).

Take a moment to look at the image of the bandolier bag (left), and reflect on the skill required to create this item and especially the beadwork. Beading designs require a comprehensive understanding of angles, dimensions, area, perimeter, geometry, exponents, data management, and so many other mathematical concepts/applications.

bandolier bag

Key Terms

regalia: clothing and apparel Indigenous peoples wear during celebrations such as powwows

identity: who someone is and the beliefs, values, history, and world-view that defines that person or his or her group

Spiritual

Beadwork is a traditional art form shared among the majority of the 500 Nations. Each Nation has its own techniques, skills, and uses for beadwork. You will see these bead patterns on clothing, regalia, and other daily-life items. Beadwork is passed down through the grandmothers and is an expression of identity. It embodies traditions, beliefs, and symbols from time immemorial.

Physical

Time: 75 minutes

Materials/Resources

- Samples of Beadwork (RM 2.1)
- Graph Paper (RM 2.2)
- *Beadwork: First Peoples' Beading History and Techniques* by Belcourt (2010), or go to: <http://nativetech.org/beadwork/beadgraph/> or <www.native-languages.org/beadwork.htm>
- computer/tablet with Internet access (optional)
- geoboards
- rubber bands
- pencil crayons (variety of colours)
- magnifying glasses
- masking tape

Considerations

- If possible, access authentic examples of beadwork to showcase from Indigenous peoples in your area.
- Do not refer to the beadwork in the past tense. Beadwork patterns and applications are still being created today.

Suggested Adaptations by Grade

9 – Solve problems involving the areas/perimeters of a variety of two-dimensional shapes, as found in local beadwork designs.

10 – Introduce the concepts, formulas, and mathematical principles related to trigonometry. Apply to a variety of beadwork designs found in the recommended book or websites.

11 – Using primary trigonometric ratios, the cosine law, and the sine law, pose problems involving a variety of triangles in three-dimensional versions of Indigenous beadwork.

12 – Perform a variety of mathematical conversions by investigating properties of complex Indigenous beadwork, using an assortment of tools and processes. Consider real-world applications, and convey.

Emotional

Learning Goal

To explore Indigenous beadwork and make connections to their mathematical innovativeness.

Step by Step

> ***Important Note!* Share the spiritual insight and the key terms as a point of reference throughout this lesson for yourself and the students.**

Minds-On

1. Give each student a magnifying glass and samples of Indigenous beadwork (RM 2.1). Have students highlight and record mathematical properties that have been discussed in class, to date, on this copy (e.g., operating with exponents, understanding characteristics of linear relations, investigating the optimal values of measurements).
2. Have students post their work on the classroom wall. As a whole class, take five minutes to review the properties identified by the students.

During

1. Show the students other examples of beadwork from the Belcourt book or one of the suggested websites.
2. Place students in pairs or triads. Give each pair or triad a geoboard along with a variety of rubber bands.
3. Ask students to examine RM 2.1 or one of the other beadwork examples (book or website). Have them recreate a symbol or shape from this beadwork and transfer it to the geoboard.
4. Allow students a maximum of 10 minutes to experiment with the beadwork examples and geoboards. Encourage them to make a series of symbols or shapes and to overlap them on their geoboard.
5. Explain to students that their geoboards represent a fixed surface area (you can choose the appropriate measurements). Their challenge is to create their own beadwork designs, which they will eventually transfer to graph paper. Allow students a maximum of 20 minutes to construct their designs.
6. Provide each student with pencil crayons and a copy of Graph Paper (RM 2.2). Have them recreate an aspect of the beadwork design they created with their partner(s). Remind them to be aware of symmetry, detail, and the use of colour. You may present other challenges that represent the curricular expectations of your province/territory.

Consolidation

Select one of the questions below to synthesize and contemporize the learning from the lesson.

- What would happen if the surface area of the beadwork changed in shape or size? How could this affect your design?
- How does this activity provide you with insight into the mathematical abilities of Indigenous peoples?
- Provide an example of how you connected trigonometry principles with a beadwork design.
- Are there other mathematical terms and concepts that can be applied to these activities?

Intellectual

Assessment

For – Recording of known mathematical properties and concepts on beadwork copy.
As – Recreation of designs or shapes with group members as peer assessors.
Of – Responses to a select question that consolidates their connection to Indigenous beadwork.

Extensions

- Invite an Indigenous resource person to the classroom, and have him or her conduct a beading workshop with your students.
- Create a digital version of a beadwork design, using software such as DynamicSketch, Dynamic Geometry, Sketchpad, or SketchUp.

Samples of Beadwork

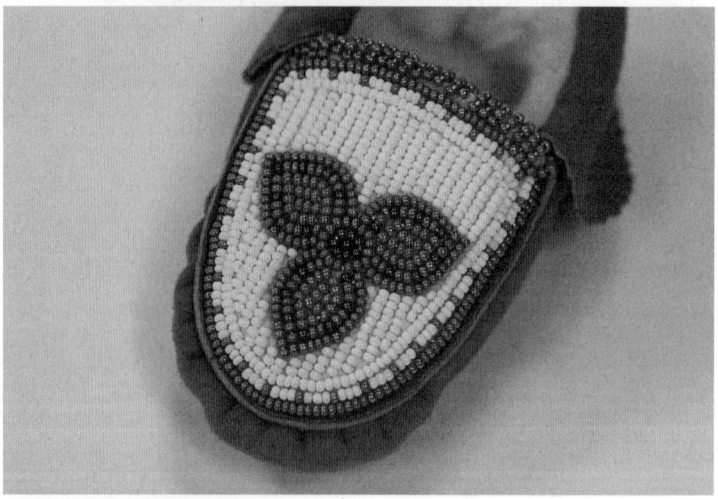

Date: ____________________ Name: ___________________________________

Graph Paper

3.0 SCIENCE LESSON PLAN

Background Information for Teachers

Indigenous Traditional Knowledge (ITK) is a term used today in the fields of environmental stewardship, earth sciences, and other related disciplines. Science from an Indigenous perspective is based upon the principles of holism, interconnectedness, and real-world applications. Western science typically is housed in mathematical theories and has well-developed deductive methodologies. Often, Western approaches to science have relegated ITK as nonscience, and this has contributed to a lack of respect for Indigenous peoples' knowledge. New science and the emerging concern for the world and human rights have resulted in the integration of ITK and Western science. Abenaki writer/researcher Cassandra Brooks (2009) carefully sums it up as a movement of "... bringing together western science and traditional knowledge [as] opening the dialogue to diverse ways of knowing." The learning goal of this lesson supports that notion and is critical in assisting students to develop a broader view of science, as well as an appreciation for the contributions of Indigenous peoples to this field.

Key Terms

Indigenous peoples: distinct groups that have an historical continuity of living on ancestral lands before precolonial and pre-invasion from settler Nations. These distinct groups have often been displaced by settler Nations; however, they are firm in the preservation of their sovereignty, world-view, lands, and traditions.

innovation: creation of something; new method, device, process, or object; usually represents a new way to do something or to enhance life

Spiritual

Indigenous peoples have made and continue to make valuable scientific contributions to the world. Many of our foods come from Indigenous Nations. On Turtle Island (North America and parts of the Mesoamericas), the 500 Nations have contributed innovations to the disciplines of architecture, agriculture, psychology, metallurgy, engineering, transportation, environmental stewardship, and so much more. You will be surprised at how your daily lives are affected by the innovations of Indigenous Nations.

Physical

Time: 75 minutes

Materials/Resources

- Task Cards (RM 3.1)
- scissors
- *Encyclopedia of American Indian Contributions to the World: 15 000 Years of Inventions and Innovations* by Keoke and Porterfield (2003), or go to: <http://sacnas.org/community/native/resources> or <www.pps.k12.or.us/depts-c/mc-me/be-ai-sc.pdf>.
- access to computer lab and Internet
- sticky notes

Considerations

- It is important to locate and present Indigenous scientific contributions through primary sources (local Indigenous Nations) and secondary sources (e.g., Keoke and Porterfield text) to your class.
- Do not disregard local Indigenous Nations and their contributions to a wider definition and understanding of science.

Suggested Adaptations by Grade

9 – Explore Earth- and space-science contributions of Indigenous peoples, with specific reference to celestial objects and/or Indigenous concepts of interconnectedness in Earth/human interactions.

10 – Develop a class-information board on Indigenous peoples' understanding of the earth's climate as dynamic and how climate has affected traditional lands and spaces. Relate these findings back to how we all are responsible for this issue.

11 – Investigate plant uses by Indigenous peoples, and connect these original ideas to the anatomy, growth, and function of plants. Highlight how such diversity in plant life is critical to Earth's ecosystems. Access a primary local resource that has the Indigenous words for local plants.

12 – Generate research in the areas of Indigenous science contributions and their connections to biochemistry, ecology, and solutions/solubility (chemistry). Highlight the importance of interdisciplinary approaches in the construction of knowledge.

Important Note! **Share the spiritual insight and the key terms as a point of reference throughout this lesson for yourself and the students.**

Emotional

Learning Goal

To make links between Indigenous science and real-world applications.

Step by Step

Minds-On

1. Give each student two sticky notes.
2. Create a class KWL chart on a large surface for all to see.
3. On the first sticky note, have students record one thing they know about Indigenous peoples contributions to science. Once completed, have students post their responses under the K on the class KWL chart.
4. As a class, review students' prior knowledge.
5. On the second sticky note, have students record one thing they would like to know about Indigenous peoples' contributions to science. Once completed, have students post their responses under the W on the class KWL chart.
6. Review these focuses for inquiry with the class.

During

1. Photocopy Task Cards (RM 3.1), and cut apart the cards. Divide the class into groups of two or three students. Give each group a task card and five sticky notes.
2. Present the Keoke/Porterfield text or the websites as one of the key resources for the task-card activities. Students can also use a search engine of their choice for more results.
3. Inform students they will be researching the task on their task card. Reinforce they are to use the hints on the card to narrow their search, and that this is a timed activity. Explain each sticky note is to be filled out by a member of the group.
4. Take the students to the computer lab, and give them 25 minutes to complete the activity on the task card.
5. When completed, bring the students back to the classroom, and have them post their responses under the L (what I have learned) on the KWL chart.
6. As a class, review the KWL chart.

Consolidation

Select one of the questions below to synthesize and contemporize the learning from the lesson.

- What are some of the impacts Indigenous peoples have had on science?

- How would you feel if your contributions were not recognized or were stolen by another? Explain.
- Can you make connections between the innovations and science principles, techniques, and knowledge you are learning about in class today?
- Where can Indigenous science and innovations have impacts on the issues facing our world?

Intellectual

Assessment

For – Completion of prior knowledge section of the class KWL chart.

As – Collaborative research among team members regarding a task-card focus.

Of – Responses to one of the questions on Indigenous contributions to the field of science.

Extensions

- Take students on an out-of-doors field trip with an Indigenous resource person for a traditional and interactive perspective on the environment.
- Create a mural of the 500 Nations and their scientific contributions to the world.

Task Cards

Architecture Your task is to locate five key facts (including images) about Indigenous peoples and "apartment complex." Your search hint is "Pueblo Bonito at Chaco Canyon."	**Metallurgy** Your task is to locate five key facts (including images) about Indigenous peoples and "smelting." Your search hints are "Moche peoples" and "Inca guayra" (a type of furnace).	**Military** Your task is to locate five key facts (including images) about Indigenous peoples and "military contributions." Your search hint is "code talkers."
Foods Your task is to locate five key facts (including images) about Indigenous peoples and "food contributions." Your search hint is "agriculture and Native Americans."	**Astronomy** Your task is to locate five key facts (including images) about Indigenous peoples and "traditional calendars." Your search hint is "ancient Native American calendar."	**Civil Engineering** Your task is to locate five key facts (including images) about Indigenous peoples and "bridges." Your search hint is "Inca simp'achaka."
Transportation Your task is to locate five key facts (including images) about Indigenous peoples and "road systems." Your search hint is "traditional road systems and Native Americans."	**Psychology** Your task is to locate five key facts (including images) about Indigenous peoples and "psychological field contributions." Your search hint is "traditional psychotherapy and Native Americans."	**Indigenous Traditional Knowledge** Your task is to locate five key facts (including images) about Indigenous peoples' contributions to science. Your search is open. Remember to approach this task with Indigenous science viewed as holistic (interdisciplinary).

4.0 HISTORY LESSON PLAN

Background Information for Teachers

Treaties are agreements that detail promises, benefits, and obligations between Nations. Treaties negotiated between Indigenous peoples and the Government of Canada were signed to define the rights of Indigenous peoples and clarify how governments (and their citizens) were to use the lands of Indigenous peoples.

There are approximately 70 recognized treaties in Canada. These treaties include historic treaties made between 1701 and 1923 and current treaties known as comprehensive land claim settlements (e.g., Nunavut).

Treaty rights refer to the specific rights of Indigenous peoples. These are affirmed in the treaties they entered into with the British government (now Canada). These treaty rights include lands set aside for exclusive use of Indigenous peoples, as well as their rights to hunt, fish, and trap on Crown land. Treaty rights are protected by subsection 35(1) of the *Constitution Act*, 1982.

Key Terms

treaty: formal and legally binding agreement between two parties. In the Canadian context, treaties are agreements between Nations – Indigenous and governmental representatives.

colonialism: form of invasion where one group subjugates or oppresses another. In the Canadian context, settler nations moved onto Indigenous lands and attempted to assimilate Indigenous Nations through various means.

Spiritual

Over 2000 treaties have been made between settler cultures' representatives in North America and Indigenous Nations since the point of contact. Not one of these treaties has been fully honoured by settler Nations. Section 35 of the Constitution acknowledges the inherent rights of Indigenous peoples and the treaties (pre- and post-Confederation). However, Indigenous peoples are the poorest in their own lands (called "fourth-world status").

Physical

Time: 75 minutes

Materials/Resources

- Treaties in Canada (RM 4.1)
- Timeline Visual Organizer (RM 4.2)
- *Aboriginal Peoples in Canada* by Reed, Elijah, and Lickers (2011), or go to: <www.thecanadianencyclopedia.ca/en/article/aboriginal-treaties/> or <http://firstpeoplesofcanada.com/fp_treaties/fp_treaties_menu.html>
- computer/tablet with Internet access (optional)
- pencil crayons
- masking tape
- deck of playing cards
- markers
- chart paper (post several sheets around the classroom)

Considerations

- Establish protocols for respectful discussion of the issues related to treaties and rights of Indigenous peoples.
- Do not single out Indigenous students and ask them for their perspective on the issues.

Suggested Adaptations by Grade

9 – Investigate the concepts of communities, conflict, and cooperation as they relate to both Indigenous peoples and non-Indigenous peoples, with specific reference to constitutional and treaty rights (difference/commonality).

10 – Investigate the concepts of identity, citizenship, and heritage as they relate to both Indigenous and non-Indigenous peoples in Canada. Focus on current movements, such as Idle No More, and the forces behind these movements.

11 – Study a key aspect of Canadian history and politics (since 1945) as it relates to Indigenous peoples and treaty issues. Focus on the main players and how these issues affect all Canadians.

12 – Engage in an investigation of Canadian and international laws as they connect to Indigenous peoples. A suggested focus is the United Nations Declaration on the Rights of Indigenous Peoples.

Emotional

Learning Goal

To value the importance of treaties as an integral part of Canadian history.

Step by Step

Minds-On

1. Provide each student with a photocopy of Treaties in Canada (RM 4.1).
2. Have students shade in all the areas on the map that are affected by treaties. Once completed, have students post their maps on a classroom wall.
3. Facilitate a brief class discussion on what students notice about the treaty map of Canada. Review their findings for common themes and differences.

Important Note! Share the spiritual insight and the key terms as a point of reference throughout this lesson for yourself and the students.

During

1. Give each student a copy of the Timeline Visual Organizer (RM 4.2). Explain they are to complete Part A during the 10-minute mini-lesson by recording the names (and numbers, if applicable) of two treaties that have piqued their interest (with the respective signing year of each and one fact for each).
2. Conduct a 10-minute mini-lesson on treaties, combining the information from Background Information for Teachers or chapter 5 of *Aboriginal Peoples in Canada* or one of the suggested websites. Focus on the treaties that correspond with your region, province/territory, and/or curriculum expectations. Ensure that the dates and key interpretations of these treaties are emphasized.
3. Upon completion of the 10-minute mini-lesson, allow students to reflect on their findings. Give them another five minutes to add any other additional information on Part A of the timeline organizer. They can confer with a buddy to do this.
4. Give each student a card from the deck of cards. Using a modified jigsaw method, have students complete Part B – the three key learnings' section of the visual organizer. For example, have each student holding a heart card find another student holding a heart card and share with each other one thing each has learned about treaties. Each can then record the point their peer has raised. Continue using this approach (card suits) until all students have collected and recorded two points about treaties. Then, have students return to their seats. There, they are to independently review the three responses and circle the one they find the most interesting.
5. Facilitate a brief discussion about the responses they found the most interesting.

Consolidation

Select one of the questions below to synthesize and contemporize the learning from the lesson.

- Is this information about treaties useful in your understanding of Indigenous peoples? How?
- What legal differences exist between Indigenous peoples and non-Indigenous peoples?
- Can you connect your understanding of Indigenous treaties to a current Indigenous issue today?
- How would history have been different/same if the treaties had been honoured by settler governments?

Intellectual

Assessment

For – Completion of map and discussion on findings.
As – Cooperative sharing of key learning(s), and completion of treaty timeline organizer.
Of – Responses to a select question that consolidates student understanding of treaties.

Extensions

- Use a case-based approach to the study of treaties. The Office of the Treaty Commission in Saskatchewan (<www.otc.ca/>) has a multitude of treaty resources, as well as the James McKay text and the Treaty 3 examples on page 124 of *Aboriginal Peoples in Canada.*
- Go to a local community (First Nations, Métis, and/or Inuit) or friendship centre to speak with Indigenous members to get their perspective on treaties.

Date: ______________________ Name: ______________________

Treaty Areas of Canada

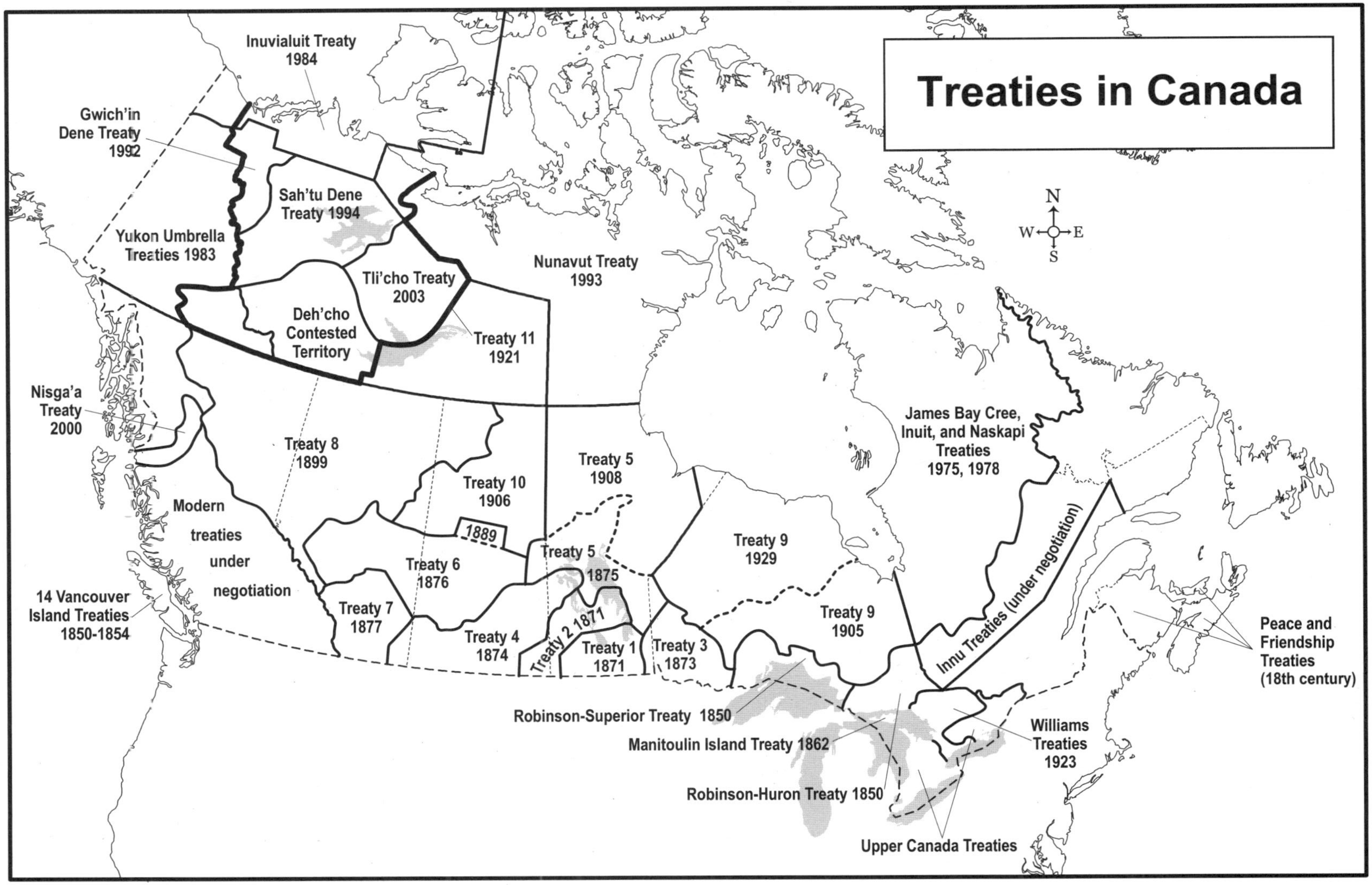

Date: ________________ Name: ____________________________

Timeline Visual Organizer

Part A

Record the names (and numbers, if applicable) of the two treaties you learned about in the mini-lesson that have piqued your interest.	Record the date (year only) of these treaties and the one fact that stands out to you about each treaty.
1.	
2.	

Part B

List three key learnings you have acquired from your peers in this exercise.

1.

2.

3.

5.0 GEOGRAPHY LESSON PLAN

Background Information for Teachers

Geography is the study of the physical features of Earth. Geography also examines humans in terms of land use, resources, and activities. Indigenous peoples on Turtle Island (North America and the Mesoamericas) have an established relationship with the land. All 500 Nations learned to live on their lands and drew upon the resources for food, housing, transportation, medicine, technology, entertainment, and other facets of life. For example, the Ojibwe who lived around the Great Lakes created birchbark canoes to navigate waterways. They did so with the materials that were plentiful and natural to their areas. Another example comes from the Inuit in Northern Canada who created portable space heaters to warm their lodges. These were made by burning animal fat at a slow rate in locally made containers. This innovation provided a sustainable source of warmth.

Key Terms

ingenuity: qualities of cleverness, talent, and resourcefulness. Ingenuity is clearly reflected in the historical and ongoing contributions of Indigenous peoples.
interdependence: complex and reciprocal relationships between people and their environments. For Indigenous peoples, this state was necessary to survival and sustenance.

Spiritual

Interdependence and reciprocity are major philosophies embedded in the world-view of Indigenous peoples. Stewardship of the environment and living in spiritual tandem with Mother Earth are part of these teachings. Indigenous peoples have always been creative in how they live and thrive in their environments.

Physical

Time: 75 minutes

Materials/Resources

- Geographical Regions of Turtle Island (RM 5.1)
- Summary Chart (RM 5.2)
- *A Native American Thought Of It: Amazing Inventions and Innovations* by Landon and MacDonald (2008), or go to: <www.american-indians.net/cultures.htm> or <www.academic.muohio.edu/his121/>

- laptop computers/tablets with Internet access (one per small group)
- chart paper
- markers
- masking tape

Considerations

- Reinforce the impact Indigenous contributions continue to have on the world, and link these contributions to students' life experiences.
- Do not freeze Indigenous peoples in the past. Offer local examples of the connections that Indigenous peoples continue to have with the land (e.g., medicines, food, traditions, celebrations, fishing, hunting, regalia).

Suggested Adaptations by Grade

9 – Investigate ways Indigenous identity is historically tied to the land. Make specific reference to adaptations with the climate, geology, vegetation, and other factors in the physical regions of Canada.

10 – Analyze the characteristics of land use (historical and present) among Indigenous and non-Indigenous Nations. Correlate these findings with current environmental issues and case studies in the media.

11 – Compare and contrast the current standards of living for Indigenous peoples and settler cultures in Canada. Evaluate with potential solutions that are respectful and long-term.

12 – Partner with a local Elder, Métis Senator, or Indigenous resource person to access traditional perspectives on Mother Earth, and connect to the earth's geographical components (lithosphere, atmosphere, hydrosphere, biosphere).

Emotional

Learning Goal

To connect Indigenous innovations to the materials/landscape of the geographical region.

Step by Step

Minds-On

Important Note! Share the spiritual insight and the key terms as a point of reference throughout this lesson for yourself and the students.

1. Divide the class into groups of three or four students. Give each group a sheet of chart paper, markers, and masking tape. Have a student in each group write *Indigenous Land* in the centre of the sheet of chart paper. Each group is then to brainstorm around the words. Let students know this is a timed activity (five minutes maximum). Reinforce there is no right or wrong way to do this. Have groups post their work upon completion.
2. As a class, spend five minutes reviewing the groups' commentaries.

During

1. Give each group a copy of Geographical Regions of Turtle Island (RM 5.1). Explain that each group will be assigned a geographical region, and its task will be to locate one innovation/invention that evolved from that region or locate one innovation/invention that came from one of the Nations located in that region.
2. Provide each small group with a laptop (with Internet connection), or take the class to the computer lab. Assign a geographical region to each group. Instruct the groups to conduct their research by having each member take a question to complete. This is a timed activity of 25 minutes.
3. Once complete, have each group prepare a final copy using the Summary Chart (RM 5.2). This is a brief exercise, as the groups have the information in draft form already. They are to post their good copy on the classroom wall with masking tape when completed.
4. Once all good copies are posted, take the students on a gallery walk to review one another's work.
5. Facilitate a brief class discussion on the findings of each group.

Consolidation

Select one of the questions below to synthesize and contemporize the learning from this lesson.

- How is this information useful (or not useful) in your understanding of Indigenous peoples?
- How would you judge the present-day significance of these innovations?
- Can you make further connections between the innovations and the land?
- How does this information change your understanding of geography?

Intellectual

Assessment

For – Group brainstorming session with Indigenous lands as the focus.
As – Completion of small-group research on Indigenous innovations and sharing of findings.
Of – Responses to a select question that consolidates the learning and geographical connections to Indigenous innovations.

Extensions

- Further investigate the local contributions of Indigenous peoples, and correlate these to the natural resources of the land.
- Map out more innovations from another sources (such as Keoke and Porterfield's 2003 *Encyclopedia of American Indian Contributions to the World).*

Date: ____________________ Name: ____________________________________

Geographical Regions of Turtle Island

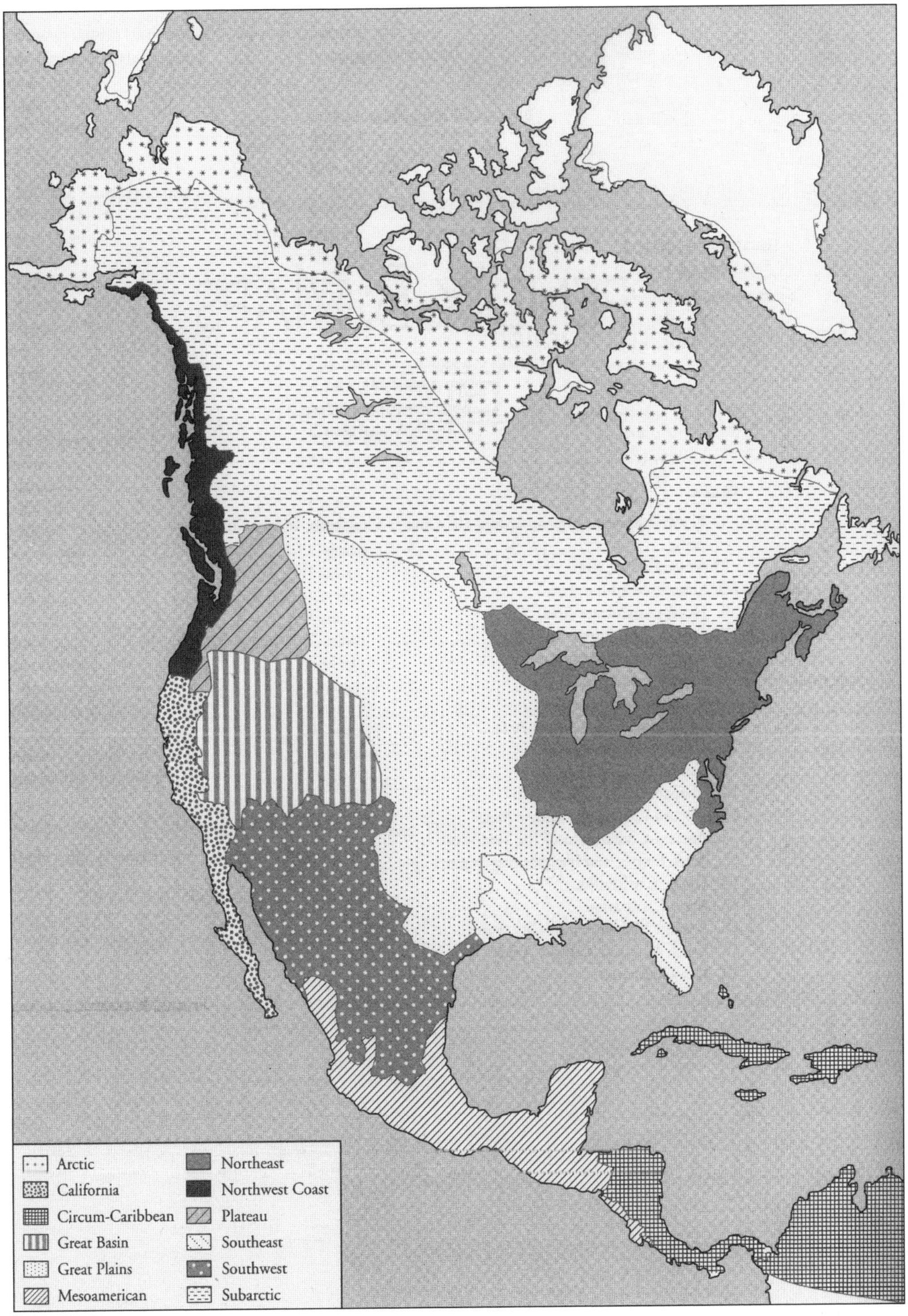

Date: ____________ Name: ____________________

Geographical Regions of Turtle Island (continued)

What region have you been assigned? ____________________

____

What source(s) will your group be using? ____________________

____

Name of your innovation/invention: ____________________

Who is credited with the innovation/invention (region or Nation)? ______

____

Describe the innovation/invention in four clear points: ____________

____

____

____

____

What does the innovation/invention look like? ____________________

____

____

____

____

____

Date: ____________________ Name: ____________________________________

Summary Chart

Geographical region: Nation(s) (if applicable):
Name of innovation/invention:
Description:
Sketch:
How do you know this innovation/invention comes from that particular geographical region? (e.g., The Ojibwe are known for their birchbark canoes. Ojibwe peoples travelled the river systems. Birchbark is plentiful in their lands. This innovation was made with local materials and served a purpose.)

6.0 HEALTH AND PHYSICAL EDUCATION LESSON PLAN

Background Information for Teachers

Indigenous games are examples of the ingenuity of Indigenous Nations; Indigenous peoples played games not only as entertainment and for health, but as a way to learn life skills. The four Indigenous games described in Information Sheet: Four Indigenous Games (RM 6.1) require very little equipment.

Three examples of traditional Indigenous games equipment are:

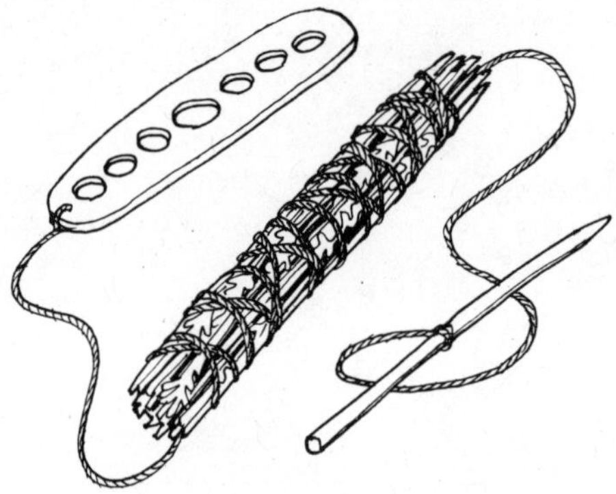

Cedar Bundle and Pin Game

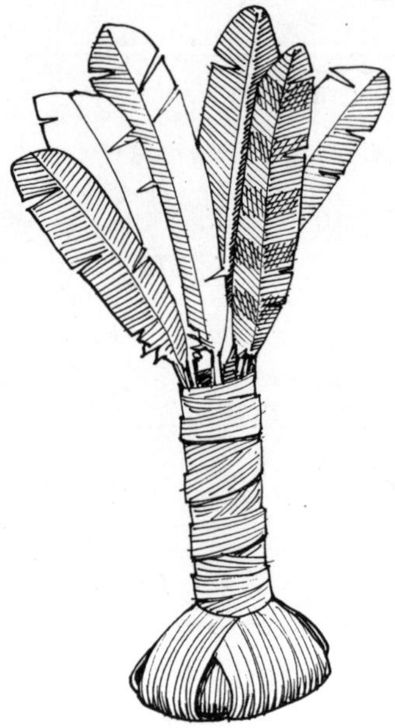

Cornhusk and Feather Shuttlecock

Birchbark Triangle and Ball Game

Key Terms

cooperation: act of working together toward a common goal or within a common set of beliefs

spiritual: sacred nature and intangible relationship that persons have with something greater than themselves

Spiritual

Indigenous games and sports are connected to the spiritual. Each game and sport has an origin story that specifies its intent and purpose. These games and sports focus on team building and the appreciation of working together in constructive competition. The sacred is always inherent in Indigenous games and sports.

Physical

Time: 75 minutes per game

Materials/Resources

- Information Sheet: Four Indigenous Games (RM 6.1)
- Indigenous Games Passport (RM 6.2)
- *Native American Games and Stories* by Bruchac and Bruchac (2000), or go to: <www.nativetech.org/games/index.php> or <http://moa.wfu.edu/files/2012/04/Fun-and-Games-Teachers-Guide.pdf>
- computer/tablet with Internet access (optional)
- basic sports equipment (based on games selected)
- gym or open field

Considerations

- Connect with local Indigenous Nations, and find out what types of traditional and contemporary sports are being played. If possible, arrange for your class to participate in a sport with that Nation.
- Do not be afraid to discuss important issues related to sports such as the controversy over "Indian" mascots and stereotypes used by some sports teams in North America.

Suggested Adaptations by Grade

9 – Focus on combining movement skills like locomotion, travelling, manipulation, and stability in select Indigenous games.

10 – Concentrate on understanding the challenges/benefits for participating in Indigenous games, both as an individual and as a member of a group or team.
11 – Explore the factors that affect full participation and understanding of Indigenous games (preparation, motivation, rules/procedures, equipment).
12 – Explain the advantages and benefits of participating in Indigenous games and the impact these games can have on improving quality of life.

Emotional

Learning Goal

To engage in traditional Indigenous games as part of health and physical education.

Step by Step

Important Note! Share the spiritual insight and the key terms as a point of reference throughout this lesson for yourself and the students.

Minds-On

1. Ask each student to think about how the spiritual insight and key terms relate to the Indigenous games they will be playing today.
2. Give each student a copy of Information Sheet: Four Indigenous Games (RM 6.1) and an Indigenous Games Passport (RM 6.2). Review the games and the tasks to be completed after each game is played. For each game, for example, students are to record two skills they have practised and one key learning related to Indigenous peoples.

During

1. Play a selection of the games described in RM 6.1 or in the Bruchac book or on one of the suggested websites. Choose the games based on the equipment and resources available at your school.
2. Review the rules of the game(s) with students. Make sure all students understand the rules.
3. Play one of the games. Take a break after 10 minutes, and have students fill in the first section of their passport (five minutes maximum).
4. Select another Indigenous game, and repeat the process (steps 2 and 3).
5. Ensure you have a cool-down component after the games.
6. Have the students briefly share with a partner the results of their passport by focusing on the game they enjoyed the most, the skills they used, and the contributions of Indigenous peoples as they understand it.

Consolidation

Select one of the questions below to synthesize and contemporize the learning from the lesson.

- What changes to these games would you recommend to accommodate a variety of diverse students?
- How can you adapt these games and still be respectful of the initial purposes?
- Can you identify the muscle groupings being used in this Indigenous game?
- Are there other motor skills you would like to see focused on as part of this game?

Intellectual

Assessment

For – Reflection on uniqueness of Indigenous games based on spiritual insight.
As – Playing games and intermittent identification of skills recorded on passport.
Of – Responses to a select question that consolidates connections to Indigenous games.

Extensions

- Use another key resource, such as *Our Original Games: A Look at Aboriginal Sport in Canada* by Bruce Miller (2008), for additional games to play.
- Organize an Indigenous sports day, and co-plan with a local Indigenous school. Use primary and secondary resources to select activities to be featured.

Four Indigenous Games

Running Game

No equipment needed. All participants line up behind a starting line. Each participant takes a deep breath. The starter yells, "Go!" The participants then start running and yelling at the same time using just the one breath. Each participant stops when that one breath has been used. The starter then checks to see who can go the farthest. The goal of this game is to gauge lung/breath capacity.

Ball Race

Each participant needs a hockey stick and tennis ball. Two goalie nets (or pylons set up to mark the goal area) are set up at opposite ends of the gym or field. Divide the class into two equal teams. Give each player a hockey stick and a tennis ball. Have the two teams line up behind their net (no goalies). The starter yells, "Go!" At the same time, each team rushes toward the other team's net and tries to score. The goal of this game is to use speed and precision to score as many points in a brief amount of time.

Shuttlecock

Give each participant a badminton shuttlecock. Divide the class into two equal teams. Each player on the team faces a partner from the opposite team with five to seven metres separating them. Let the teams know that this is a timed activity (five minutes). The starter yells, "Go!" Each participant tries to keep his or her shuttlecock in the air using only one hand as a modified racquet. Once the participant drops the shuttlecock, he or she sits down on the spot. The goal of the game is to have the most participants on the team standing at the end of the five minutes. The time can be increased as the skill of the teams increases.

Crab Race

Only a starting line and finishing line are needed for this game (length is up to the starter). Have all participants line up at the starting line with two metres separating each player. The starter yells, "Go!" Each participant drops onto all fours (but reversed, with the back facing the ground) and starts crawling toward the finish line. The starter can tell participants to change the direction of the crawl (e.g., move sideways, move forwards with feet toward the finish line, move backwards with feet facing the starting line). The goal of this game is dexterity.

Date: ________________ Name: ____________________________

Indigenous Games Passport

Name of game	Record two skills needed to play this game	Record one thing you learned about this Indigenous game
1.		
2.		
3.		
4.		

7.0 DRAMA LESSON PLAN

Background Information for Teachers

Indigenous legends offer all communities insights into a diverse world of perspectives about life in the past, present, and future. There are legends about love, fear, humility, humour, and others about the mysterious/supernatural (e.g., Creation, Bigfoot, Space, Shapeshifters). The genres and topics of legends from Indigenous Nations are endless. Some legends are so sacred they cannot be recorded, or they can only be retold in a particular setting by a particular storyteller. Other legends serve as teachings on living a good life. For example, in the Great Lakes Indigenous territories, there are many legends about "how things came to be." Legends about "the first strawberries" or "rainbow crow" or "old man winter" help us to gain a new view and understanding of the beings that co-exist on Mother Earth. Rainbow Crow, for instance, comes from the Lenape peoples and explains how the Crow turned black in colour. This legend teaches us about self-sacrifice and love.

Key Terms

tableau: drama technique in which participants freeze and make a still image of a scene or a moment in a story

legend: traditional story handed down between generations, usually in oral form. A variety of purposes and functions is embedded in the story.

Spiritual

Indigenous Nations have many legends that serve a variety of purposes and functions. These legends offer insight into the world-view, history, and traditions of Indigenous peoples. Each Nation has its own protocols for telling legends; however, the listener has equal responsibility in this sacred process.

Physical

Time: 75 minutes

Materials/Resources

- Insights Organizer (RM 7.1), or go to: <www.firstpeople.us/FP-Html-Legends/Legends-AB.html> or <www.native-languages.org/legends.htm>
- computer/tablet with Internet access (optional)
- large space for movement
- chart paper
- markers

- masking tape
- pens/pencils

Considerations

- Reinforce the importance of respecting both one another's space and interpretations of the legends.
- Do not be afraid to discuss Indigenous stereotypes present in popular culture (e.g., warrior, Pocahontas) and why such stereotypes can be dehumanizing.

Suggested Adaptations by Grade

9 – Describe the themes, ideas, characters, feelings, and beliefs emerging from the legend through further exploration and representation.
10 – Identify an alternate form to present the legend, and discuss the impact of this dramatic medium (e.g., radio, video).
11 – Analyze the legend and a variety of other Indigenous legends to understand how ideas and beliefs about Indigenous issues and cultures are transmitted.
12 – Generate ideas for how Indigenous legends, through public performances and productions, can bridge universal themes that exist among diverse cultures.

Emotional

Learning Goal

To explore Indigenous legends and express with tableau as the primary dramatic art form.

Step by Step

Minds-On

1. Have students form a large circle. Instruct them to take a large step back so they have lots of personal space between themselves and their peers.
2. Engage them in a form of tableau that focuses on the seasons. As springboards for movement, have them assume poses on topics such as favourite winter sport or activity or favourite summer weather.
3. Display a sheet of chart paper, and title it "Indigenous Legends." Give each student a marker. On the posted chart paper, have each student record a key word he or she believes relates to Indigenous legends. This will provide insight into prior learning of the topic.
4. As a class, review the key words.

Important Note! **Share the spiritual insight and the key terms as a point of reference throughout this lesson for yourself and the students.**

During

1. Have students return to the circle and sit down.
2. Select one of the shorter legends from the suggested websites, and read aloud to the class. This should take a maximum of 10 minutes.
3. Give each student a copy of Insights Organizer (RM 7.1). Review the tasks on the organizer, and inform the students they will complete this organizer toward the end of this lesson.
4. Have students stand up again and take a large step back for personal space.
5. Conduct another tableau session, using lines from the legend you have already selected and read. Select simple examples from the legend students can do individually; then, move onto more complex examples that involve students teaming up.
6. Conclude the legend/tableau session by giving students five minutes to complete the Insights Oganizer.
7. Facilitate a brief session where students can share one aspect of their Insights Organizer (RM 7.1).

Consolidation

Select one of the questions to synthesize and contemporize the learning from the lesson.

- What are the underlying themes in the legend?
- Do you believe legends offer a new connection to the natural world? Why or why not?
- How can you apply the teachings in these legends to a situation in your world?
- Can you connect other dramatic skills/forms/knowledge to this legend?

Intellectual

Assessment

For – Recording and reviewing key words associated with legends.

As – Performing aspects of the legend in tableau mode and discussion at end.

Of – Responses to a select question that consolidates understanding of the selected legend.

Extensions

- Take the legend to the next level by planning and implementing a full-play production.
- Take one of the legends from the suggested websites, and reproduce this activity using the same process with a new dramatic technique. Compare important insights.

Date: ____________________ Name: ________________________________

Insights Organizer

Tableau was (or was not) an effective drama method for interpreting these legends:	
This is what I have learned about Indigenous peoples:	
This is what I have learned about myself and my peers:	

8.0 MUSIC LESSON PLAN

Background Information for Teachers

Indigenous music and Indigenous history are deeply embedded together. The stories, traditions, and values of Indigenous peoples are often told through songs. Music is an integral part of the ceremonies and celebrations of Indigenous peoples.

Traditional musical instruments of Indigenous peoples reflect the availability of materials in their lands. For example, in the Great Lakes/Woodlands area, drums, rattles, striking sticks, whistles, and flutes are primary instruments made from the flora and fauna of the area. A call-and-response style (antiphony) is traditional to these territories and the people. In the Arctic, box drums and throat singing are traditional. Throat singing is a form of vocalizing that is recitative and complex, and is found in very few cultures in the world.

Contemporary Indigenous music is diverse, and the genres mastered by Indigenous peoples are broad.

Key Terms

musical genre: category applied to a piece of music identifiable by distinguishable techniques, styles, content, and context

Hip-hop: style of music featuring rap as the primary feature. It has its roots in African-American culture and is known for its stylistic features of emceeing, scratching records, break dancing, and graffiti art.

Spiritual

Music is an integral part of the cultures and world-views of the 500 Nations on Turtle Island. Each Nation is known for a particular genre rooted in its history. Contemporary Indigenous music carries messages of resilience, pride, teachings, traditions, and the stories of the peoples.

Physical

Time: 75 minutes

Materials/Resources

- Musical Connections Organizer (RM 8.1)
- access to website: <http://nativehiphop.net/>
- access to website: <http://aboriginalmusiccountdown.ca/stations/>
- access to website: <www.last.fm/tag/native%20american>
- computer/tablet with Internet access

- variety of markers
- chart paper
- masking tape

Considerations

- Include local Indigenous music as part of this lesson. Using a resource available to you, locate a variety of genres to play for the students.
- Encourage students to identify other Indigenous artists who are important or to whom they have access.

Suggested Adaptations by Grade

9 – Focus on researching the music, musicians, and critics' opinions about Indigenous music. Describe the impacts this information has on Indigenous and non-Indigenous peoples.

10 – Identify the skills, habits, and values nurtured in the process of creating music. Demonstrate these findings by researching an Indigenous musician (biography).

11 – Drawing upon the techniques of score study and purposeful listening, critique the elements in a select song by an Indigenous musician. Offer variations to the composition.

12 – Assess the impact of Indigenous music, Indigenous musicians, and various genres on students' self-awareness, knowledge of social issues, and expansion of musical techniques and methods.

Emotional

Learning Goal

To make personal connections and meanings with select Indigenous music.

Step by Step

Important Note! *Share the spiritual insight and the key terms as a point of reference throughout this lesson for yourself and the students.*

Minds-On

1. Give students a variety of markers.
2. Play one of the music videos from <http://nativehiphop.net/>.
3. At the end of the video, briefly discuss, as a class, the messages and images that emerged from this Indigenous hip-hop music video.
4. Tape the chart paper to the wall, and have each student write a message or draw an image on it to show what stood out for him or her in the video.
5. Briefly review the messages/images presented by the students.

During

1. Give each student a copy of Musical Connections Organizer (RM 8.1). As a class, review the tasks (listen, reflect, write).
2. Select one of the radio stations or songs from the websites in the resource list. Play a song, and then give the students five minutes to complete the first section of RM 8.1. Repeat this process with two other songs.
3. Give students five minutes to share RM 8.1 with a partner.
4. Instruct students to take a marker and, on the chart paper taped to the wall, write or draw the meanings/images they associate with the Indigenous music.
5. Facilitate a brief discussion about students' meanings/images.

Consolidation

Select one of the questions below to synthesize and contemporize the learning from the lesson.

- Can you identify and describe other musical pieces/arrangements similar to an Indigenous genre studied today?
- What are some of the other meanings behind Indigenous music?
- How can the Indigenous music heard today be further applied to musical theory you are learning in class?
- How would you alter a piece of Indigenous music heard today in a creative manner?

Intellectual

Assessment

For – Drawing images and/or writing meanings from the Indigenous hip-hop video.
As – Completion of organizer, and sharing with a partner.
Of – Responses to a select question that connects Indigenous music to learning from the lesson.

Extensions

- As a class, attend a local powwow to experience the variety and complexity of drumming (large drums and hand drums) and rattles.
- Bring in a local Indigenous resource person to the classroom to conduct a workshop on creating a musical composition representative of the area.

Date: ____________________ Name: ____________________________

Musical Connections Organizer

Song #1 Title and Artist:	Reflect on what you are learning in music class (genres, theory, skills, notes, other). Connect one thing you are learning in class with this Indigenous piece of music. Describe in two points. 1. 2.
Song #2 Title and Artist:	Reflect on what you are learning in music class (genres, theory, skills, notes, other). Connect one thing you are learning in class with this Indigenous piece of music. Describe in two points. 1. 2.
Song #3 Title and Artist:	Reflect on what you are learning in music class (genres, theory, skills, notes, other). Connect one thing you are learning in class with this Indigenous piece of music. Describe in two points. 1. 2.

9.0 VISUAL ARTS LESSON PLAN

Background Information for Teachers

Archaeologists have documented Indigenous art in Northwestern Canada from the end of the last ice age, approximately 11 500 years ago. Although these artifacts are considered to be limited in detail and complexity, they are nonetheless forms of Indigenous art (Canadian Encyclopedia n.d.).

Detailed art pieces have been dated to 5000 years ago and have been found in various regions of Canada. Each Indigenous Nation is known for its traditional method of artistic expression, skill, and knowledge. For example, in the Great Lakes region, the Ojibwe are renowned for their quill boxes. These vary in design and colour:

The Haida of the Northwest are known for their carved bone items (see left).

Key Terms

symmetry: exactly corresponding parts facing each other on a central axis; mirror image

expression: taking ones thoughts and emotions and making them known in some form(s)

Spiritual

Art in traditional Indigenous societies was always related to some sort of function in life (e.g., document a hunt, please the spirits). Each artifact (art form) had a use, a story, a teaching, a process, and a creator. Contemporary Indigenous art has similar purposes and most often recreates and transmits living history and symbology.

Physical

Time: 75 minutes

Materials/Resources

- Symmetry Design (RM 9.1)
- copy or copies of images of traditional or contemporary Indigenous art from <www.historymuseum.ca/cmc/exhibitions/tresors/ethno/etb0000e.shtml> (for each student)
- *First Nations Art Projects and Activities* by Dick and Clark (1999), or go to: <www.curriculum.org/storage/258/1334331418/Exploring_Aboriginal_Art_in_Canada.pdf> or <www.maei-ppw.ca/exemplary_classroom_practice.html>
- mirrors
- magnifying glasses
- Graph Paper (see RM 2.2, page 85)
- computer/tablet with Internet access (optional)
- pencils, pencil crayons
- masking tape

Considerations

- Include a variety of images and examples of local Indigenous art for students to hold, examine, and discuss.
- Do not avoid conversations related to the commercialization of Indigenous art and symbols. Highlight, for example, how the mass production of dream-catchers (commonly available in dollar stores) is a prime example of this phenomenon.

Suggested Adaptations by Grade

9 – Explore elements of Indigenous art (e.g., colour, texture, space), and apply elements in the creation of personal artworks that convey select feelings and emotions.

10 – Experiment with a variety of other media (e.g., paint, tissue paper, charcoal, photos) when analyzing and creating personal art with an Indigenous influence.

11 – Apply Indigenous artistic elements and other principles of design in the creation of personal art pieces that communicate a social-justice issue related to Indigenous peoples.

12 – Create a class installation piece that focuses on the inclusion of alternative media and respect for the other senses (e.g., music, scent). This installation piece is to be embedded with Indigenous influences.

Emotional

Learning Goal

To explore design elements of Indigenous art and create a symmetrical piece based on these examples.

Step by Step

Minds-On

1. Distribute a copy (or copies) of Indigenous art, a mirror, and a magnifying glass to each student.
2. Explain to students they have 10 minutes to examine the art closely, using the magnifying glass and the mirror to look for symmetrical patterns.
3. Engage students in a five-minute whole-class discussion on their findings (e.g., patterns, symmetry, symbols, techniques, colour, scale).

Important Note! Share the spiritual insight and the key terms as a point of reference throughout this lesson for yourself and the students.

During

1. Display and review Indigenous art examples from the Dick and Clark book or from one of the suggested websites. Point out how this art represents an excellent example(s) of symmetry.

2. Give each student a sheet of graph paper and a pencil.
3. Have students create a basic symmetrical shape similar to one explored in the Minds-On or During section of this lesson.
4. Instruct students to continually fold the graph paper to ensure the shape is truly symmetrical.
5. Facilitate a class discussion on symmetry and the connection to the art of Indigenous peoples.
6. Give each student a copy of Symmetry Design (RM 9.1), and, as a class, review what is required to complete this task. Have students create an enhanced design of the shape they have already drawn. They are to use pencil crayons to complete this task and colour in the shape.
7. Have students post their completed work, and facilitate a gallery walk showcasing their enhanced designs.

Consolidation

Select one of the questions below to synthesize and contemporize the learning from the lesson.

- Were you able to apply some of these artistic methods to your work? How?
- Compare these examples of Indigenous art. How are they similar? How are they different?
- Can you think of other artists or works that model the techniques of these selections of Indigenous art?
- How does this exercise embody the art principles, theory, skills, and knowledge you are learning today?

Intellectual

Assessment

For – Examination and discussion of Indigenous art and properties of symmetry.
As – Sharing students' symmetrical art based upon design elements of Indigenous art.
Of – Responses to a select question that consolidates the students' learning about Indigenous art and design elements.

Extensions

- Try the sun design paper folds found in *First Nations Art Projects and Activities*. Experiment with this technique, and create other types of paper folds.
- Go to a local exhibition of Indigenous artists, or bring in an Indigenous resource person to offer a workshop that focuses on that resource persons' art techniques.

Date: ____________________ Name: ___________________________________

Symmetry Design

My design:
The Indigenous art form that has influenced my creation (what and why):
The symbolic meaning and/or messages that my design represents:

 ISBN: 978-1-55379-656-5

10.0 TECHNOLOGICAL STUDIES LESSON PLAN

Background Information for Teachers

Traditional transportation, communication practices, green businesses, construction techniques, health care, and other Indigenous industries were shared with settlers in North America. Indigenous peoples taught newcomers how to live on the land and survive in harsh areas. For example, the Inuit technologies of snow goggles, snowshoes, and shelter helped early explorers to survive/thrive in the Arctic. Also, Anishinaabe copper (especially cups) was a highly valued mined and smelted technology for trade. Health care remedies (e.g., tea of ground coniferous needles and bark for scurvy) were also shared with settlers to treat and cure disease. The picture below shows the Anishinaabe traditional industry of maple syrup and sugaring.

Anishinaabe women are making birchbark containers for maple sap.

Key Terms

technological education: study of particular industries and how they affect our daily lives. These industries include communications, computer technology, construction, green businesses, hairstyling/aesthetics, health care, tourism/hospitality, manufacturing, design, and transportation.

industry: specific branch, business, or economy defined by its products, services, and goods

Spiritual

Technology and some forms of industry have always existed within the activities of the 500 Nations on Turtle Island. Each Nation was known for its particular good(s), service(s), and/or product(s). For example, the Anishinaabe of the Great Lakes were great manufacturers of maple syrup and maple sugar (as well as traders and exporters of these products).

Physical

Time: 75 minutes

Materials/Resources

- WebQuest Organizer (RM 10.1)
- access to computers/tablets or computer lab with Internet access
- access to the Innovation, Science and Economic Development Canada website (Go to: <www.ic.gc.ca/eic/site/icgc.nsf/eng/h_07063.html>.)
- access to the Industry Canada Aboriginal Business Directory website (Go to: <www.ic.gc.ca/app/ccc/sld/cmpny.do?tag=248&profileId=381&lang=eng>.)
- access to the Indigenous and Northern Affairs Canada National WebSite (Go to: <www.aadnc-aandc.gc.ca/eng/1100100010002/1100100010021>.)
- access to your school or board website (secondary courses)
- pencils and pens

Considerations

- Present names of local Indigenous industries defined by their technologies (products and services). Be sure to highlight the Indigenous community from where the industry originates (e.g., Kahnawake Motors).
- Use the term that a community uses (e.g., Anishinaabe, Métis, Haudenosaunee) rather than the more generic and nonspecific terms *Aboriginal* and *Indigenous*.

Suggested Adaptations by Grade

9 – Identify the correct terminology that relates to a particular Indigenous industry by focusing on the tools, equipment, processes, and products of the industry.

10 – Explore the career opportunities and professional practices (including standards and ethics) and organizations associated with a particular Indigenous industry.

11 – Link a variety of Indigenous industries to technological trends, and analyze individual achievements. Investigate career opportunities.

12 – Develop relationships with Indigenous industry professionals, and plan an Indigenous career day for your students and the community. Have each student take on a role by partnering with a specific industry person for this event (i.e., invite and be the initial contact person).

Emotional

Learning Goal

To make connections between Indigenous industries and mainstream technologies.

Step by Step

Important Note! Share the spiritual insight and the key terms as a point of reference throughout this lesson for yourself and the students.

Minds-On

1. View one of the short videos on Indigenous Youth Success Stories found on the Aboriginal Affairs website at this link: <www.aadnc-aandc.gc.ca/eng/1342530987359/1342531019196>. As a class, discuss how the video is an example of the positive (and maybe negative) impact of industry.

During

1. Give each student a copy of WebQuest Organizer (RM 10.1). Assign each student an industry category to research (Part A). Review the tasks with the students (i.e., description of the industry and providing examples of these industries).
2. In the computer lab, have the students begin their WebQuest (for Part B and Part C) at the Innovation, Science and Economic Development Canada website: <www.ic.gc.ca/eic/site/icgc.nsf/eng/h_07063.html>.
3. Have students access the website Industry Canada – Aboriginal Business Directory or Indigenous and Northern Affairs Canada (to complete Part D) of their WebQuest at: <www.ic.gc.ca/app/ccc/sld/cmpny.do?tag=248&profileId=381&lang=eng> or <www.aadnc-aandc.gc.ca/eng/1100100010002/1100100010021>.

4. Provide the link to your school or school board's website to complete Part E of the WebQuest.
5. Give students 20 minutes to research the websites, then have them share their findings with a partner.
6. Back in the classroom, have students share their findings with the rest of the class.

Consolidation

Select one of the questions below to synthesize and contemporize the learning from the lesson.

- How can you distinguish between the various industries being researched? What makes each industry unique?
- How has your understanding of Indigenous peoples been (or not been) enhanced by your research?
- What technological trends are Indigenous industries leading in Canada?
- Why is researching and promoting Indigenous industries vital to building relationships between citizens?

Intellectual

Assessment

For – Review of the key terms and a discussion about the success story in the video is an example of a community affected by industry.
As – Completion of WebQuest organizer (RM 10.1) and sharing key findings with a partner.
Of – Responses to a select question and correlation to technological education.

Extensions

- Partner with Northern College and District School Board Ontario North East for their Lightning Trail program. This is a one-week summer institute for Indigenous youth that introduces them to various trades. For more information, go to <www.northernc.on.ca/>.
- Conduct a field trip or virtual site visit to an Indigenous community that operates an industry such as mining, tourism, green industries, health care, and so on.

Date: ____________ Name: ______________________

WebQuest Organizer

Part A

Circle the industry category you have been assigned by your teacher:

communications	computer technology
construction	green businesses
hairstyling/aesthetics	health care
tourism/hospitality	manufacturing
design	transportation

Part B

Describe the key features of this type of industry in two to three points:

Part C

Provide one example of this industry in your region and/or province/territory:

Part D

Provide one example of this industry that is Indigenous owned:

Part E

Are there technological education courses at your secondary school that have a focus on the industry you have been assigned? Give an example of a course (code and description).

11.0 BUSINESS STUDIES LESSON PLAN

Background Information for Teachers

Economic development is regarded as one of the primary tools to bring an enhanced quality of life to Indigenous peoples. Nine thousand First Nations citizens in the province of Ontario have their own businesses and deliver products/services to a wide range of clients and markets. According to the Canadian Council on Business (CCAB), each of these businesses experiences profitability of approximately 100 thousand dollars annually. Those businesses that have business plans in place are more likely to succeed and innovate/modernize (i.e., updating equipment and technologies, or expanding). Many Indigenous business owners are harnessing social media and e-commerce as consistent means for promoting and selling goods/services. There are 395 business profiles at the CCAB website operated by Indigenous peoples or committed to Indigenous communities and partnerships. Indigenous businesses face the same issues as other mainstream ones and are faced with the same ethical dilemmas. For example, Indigenous companies have earned just over eight billion dollars over the course of 14 years in the oil sands industry. These monies assist in building up Indigenous communities, but, at the same time, raise questions about environmental responsibility/stewardship.

Key Terms

entrepreneur: individual who starts a business or develops an idea into a business. Usually possesses vision and the ability to successfully take on an enterprise.

marketing: the activities and processes for communicating and delivering valued products and services

Spiritual

A number of Indigenous businesses across Turtle Island are models of successful practices. Many of these are connected to ethics, processes, and the delivery of services that are culturally unique. Indigenous entrepreneurs are on the rise and have harnessed the potential of e-commerce as a way to lead this growing field.

Physical

Time: 75 minutes

Materials/Resources

- Indigenous Businesses Research Chart (RM 11.1)
- access to computer lab and Internet
- pens
- access to CBC Aboriginal Main Page (Go to: <www.cbc.ca/news/aboriginal>.)
- access to Canadian Council for Aboriginal Business Membership Directory (Go to: <www.ccab.com/member-directory>.)

Considerations

- Use primary (and local) Indigenous business resources in the classroom (i.e., site visits, guest speakers, examples of products/services). This type of firsthand experience cannot be duplicated by secondary resources.
- Do not be afraid to share with your students that this exploration of Indigenous businesses and knowledge is (or may be) new to you. Taking a risk with your students shows your commitment to new learning.

Suggested Adaptations by Grade

9 – Identify the different types of businesses, forms of ownership, and the motivations for business choices made by Indigenous entrepreneurs.

10 – Explore the business communications tools (i.e., marketing, advertising, social media) an Indigenous entrepreneur is using. Analyze these tools in terms of their effectiveness and clarity.

11 – Create an online class tool kit (contacts, resources, business plans) of Indigenous entrepreneurs that highlights the entrepreneurs' ideas, opportunities for growth, potential, benefits of their products/services and innovativeness.

12 – Assemble an Indigenous entrepreneurship information kit that focuses on venture planning, e-commerce, and best practices that exist in Canada today (Canadian Council for Aboriginal Business is a good starting point).

Emotional

Learning Goal

To explore Indigenous businesses and make personal connections.

Step by Step

Minds-On

1. Select and view a short, current video related to Indigenous businesses at the CBC Aboriginal website. Show to students.
2. Guide the students in taking a pathways walk to share information with one another. During a pathways walk, students move in the classroom according to directions given by the teacher (e.g., move one large step and two small steps in any direction). When students stop, have them share with the person(s) closest to them what they learned from the video. Continue the pathways sharing for three or four more sessions. This activity should not take longer than five minutes.

During

1. Give each student a copy of the Indigenous Businesses Research Chart (RM 11.1). Review the tasks with students.
2. Take students to the computer lab, and have them link to the Canadian Council for Aboriginal Business Membership Directory website. There, have students select a business that interests them. They can then go to the business's website and complete the research organizer.
3. As students work on this activity, go around the room and survey their progress.
4. Once students have completed their research, return to the classroom, and have a brief class discussion about their findings.

Consolidation

Select one of the questions below to synthesize and contemporize the learning from the lesson.

- What are some of the motives behind these entrepreneurs and business persons?
- Are you interested (or not interested) in these particular businesses? Explain why or why not.
- How are these Indigenous businesses models of exemplary practice?
- Can you relate to one of the entrepreneurs discussed by you or your peers? Why?

***Important Note!* Share the spiritual insight and the key terms as a point of reference throughout this lesson for yourself and the students.**

Intellectual

Assessment

For – View video on Indigenous businesses, and have students share their learning, using a pathways method.
As – Completion of research organizer and checking of each student's progress.
Of – Responses to a select question about connections to Indigenous peoples and their businesses.

Extensions

- Go to a local Indigenous business for primary research and relationship-building opportunities.
- Create a business plan that focuses on partnerships with Indigenous communities.

Date: ____________ Name: ______________________

Indigenous Businesses Research Chart

Name of Indigenous business:	
Address:	
What type of business is this? Circle the description(s) that apply:	
service	retail
manufacturing	profit
not for profit	crown
public	private
other:	
What form of business ownership applies here? Circle the description(s) that apply:	
sole proprietorship	partnership
corporation	cooperative
franchise	other:
Identify and record four facts about this business that stand out for you.	
1.	
2.	
3.	
4.	

12.0 INDIGENOUS WORLD-VIEW LESSON PLAN

Background Information for Teachers

Each Indigenous Nation has its own calendar to document activities that occur within a particular season and/or lunar or solar period. The Anishinaabe of the Great Lakes have a calendar based upon 13 moons. The cycle of each moon is 28 days. This means that an Anishinaabe year is actually 364 days. There are three moons in the spring, three moons in the summer, three moons in the fall, and four moons in the winter. Each moon provides multiple teachings for people to reflect on and act upon. (If the teachings of all the moons were written down, we would have volumes of encyclopedias for each moon.) Instead, the following give a couple of examples of teachings for each moon:

- Season of Spring – Sugar Moon (a time of working together and fasting), Sucker Moon (a time of honouring our roles and humility), Flower Moon (a time of diversity and life)
- Season of Summer – Strawberry Moon (a time of kindness and giving), Raspberry/Blueberry Moon (a time of setting boundaries and renewal), Grain Moon (a time of preparation and industry)
- Season of Fall – Corn Moon (a time of appreciating uniqueness and learning), Falling Leaves Moon (a time of celebrating Mother Earth and colour), Freezing Moon (a time of dreaming and visions)
- Season of Winter – Little Spirit Moon (a time of ancestral teachings and looking inward), Big Spirit Moon (a time of doing inner work and healing), Spirit Moon (a time of silence and prayer), Bear Moon (a time of inner stirring and protection)

It is critical that an individual's interpretation of the moon teachings be respected. The listener has the responsibility to act on the teachings in a positive and personal manner.

Key Terms

world-view: perspective from which one sees and interprets the universe. Refers to the fundamental beliefs about life and existence.

Elder: highly respected person known by the Indigenous community as a celebrated knowledge person who has earned this designation. This same description applies to the term *Métis Senator.*

Spiritual

There are 500 Nations on Turtle Island, each with its own distinct world-views, traditions, values, and languages. In times gone by, all Nations had a calendar of some type. The calendar represented the activities that occurred in each season and/or lunar (or solar) cycle. Those calendars came from observing the land and were embedded with a comprehensive understanding of how to live a good life.

Physical

Time: 75 minutes

Materials/Resources

- Anishinaabe Calendar (RM 12.1)
- *Aboriginal Beliefs, Values and Aspirations* by Pearson and GoodMinds (2011), or go to: <www.thecanadianencyclopedia.ca/en/article/aboriginal-people/> or <www.native-languages.org/home.htm>
- computer/tablet with Internet access (optional)
- pencil crayons
- chart paper
- markers
- masking tape

Considerations

- Explore the types of calendars used by the Indigenous peoples in your area. Many different Nations may use different symbols to represent their understanding of the land and seasons. In this lesson, however, students will use the turtle symbol.
- Do not stop students from expressing themselves with symbols instead of text (words, sentences) in the activities. As long as they are able to orally explain the symbols, this form of literacy is valued.

Suggested Adaptations by Grade

9 – Focus on the characteristics that make up identity within an Indigenous group. Identify the symbols and connections to land that emerge from that group.
10 – Compare and contrast the cultural characteristics between various Indigenous Nations in Canada. Make connections to personal world-views held by students.

11 – Develop further understanding(s) of how Indigenous Nations' customs, practices, and beliefs are essential to identity. Elaborate on the significance of these customs as critical to public appreciation of Indigenous uniqueness.
12 – Research and describe traditional leadership practices of various Indigenous Nations. Relate this to current self-government practices that exist today by identifying cultural protocols that are unique.

Emotional

Learning Goal

To reflect on and explore the teachings of the Anishinaabe calendar.

Step by Step

Important Note! Share the spiritual insight and the key terms as a point of reference throughout this lesson for yourself and the students.

Minds-On

1. Place students into small groups of three to five. Give each group a sheet of chart paper and markers. Have a student in each group write the keyword "world-view" in the centre of the chart paper. Give students five minutes to brainstorm words, symbols, questions, and concepts related to the keyword and write their responses around the keyword.
2. Once completed, have the groups display their charts on the wall. Give each group a minute to share its interpretations and findings with the class.

During

1. Give each student a copy of the Anishinaabe Calendar (RM 12.1) and a variety of pencil crayons.
2. Instruct students to colour the large sections on the turtle's back numbered 1 to 3 yellow, the sections 4 to 6 red, the sections 7 to 9 black, and the sections 10 to 13 white (see Part A).
3. Have students record (using a legend or method of their choice) the following information on their Anishinaabe Calendar: yellow = spring, red = summer, black = fall, white = winter.
4. Explain you are now going to conduct a mini-lesson on the topic of the Anishinaabe calendar and Indigenous world-views. This mini-lesson, which is to be given orally by you (the teacher), is a listening lesson for the students. Refer to Background Information for Teachers; the text *Aboriginal Beliefs, Values and Aspirations* (sections "The Turtle Calendar" and "The Living Earth"); and/or one of the websites to conduct your mini-lesson about the 13 moons.
5. Have students listen carefully and record one teaching, fact, or other learning on their Anishinaabe calendar (see Part B). Emphasize to the students there is no wrong way to do this.

6. Use an adapted jigsaw method to divide the class into pairs of students (e.g., students who were born in the winter share with another winter person, spring with spring, summer with summer, and fall with fall).
7. Conclude by having students share their work and key learnings with their partner.

Consolidation

Select one of the questions below to synthesize and contemporize the learning from the lesson.

- Compare your world-view to that of one group of Indigenous peoples. How is it similar? How is it different?
- Why do you think changes to traditional Indigenous calendars occurred?
- What are some of the personal connections you have made to a particular moon or season in this activity?
- How is this activity an example of Indigenous Studies? Explain.

Intellectual

Assessment

For – Brainstorming session by small groups on the term *world-view.*
As – Completion of visual organizer and using a variety of methods to share information.
Of – Responses to a select question that personalizes Indigenous calendars.

Extensions

- Invite an Elder or Métis Senator to the classroom to share his or her perspective on Indigenous world-view and the teachings he or she lives by.
- Conduct a series of activities from the book, *Aboriginal Beliefs, Values and Aspirations.*

Date: ____________________ Name: ________________________________

Anishinaabe Calendar

The traditional Anishinaabe calendar is 13 moons. Each moon is 28 days. This means an Anishinaabe year is 364 days. It is said in legends that the Anishinaabe calendar was given to the people on the back of a turtle. The turtle's back has 13 large sections. The turtle also has 28 smaller sections to reflect the cycle of one moon (13 x 28 = 364 days in an Anishinaabe year).

Part A

Colour the back of the turtle as instructed by your teacher.

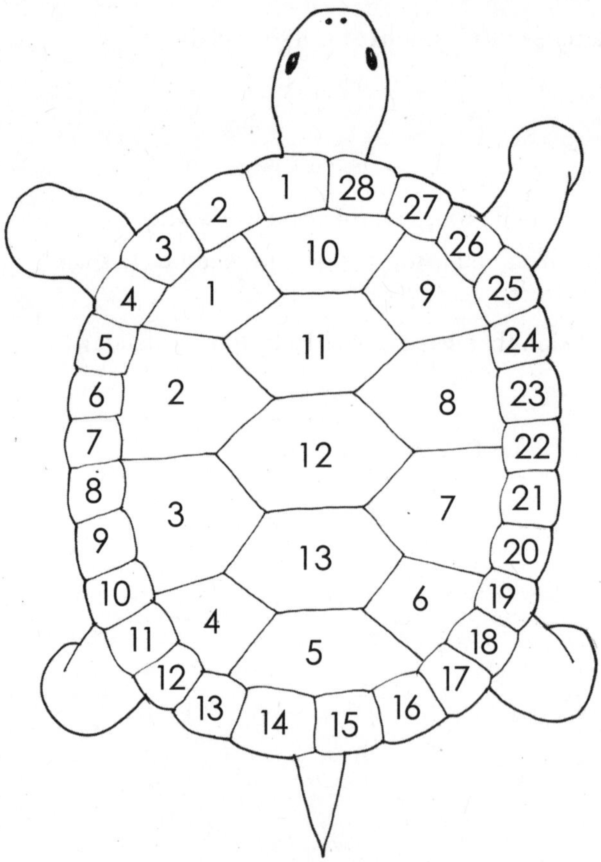

LEGEND:

Date: ____________________ Name: ____________________________________

Anishinaabe Calendar (continued)

Part B

As you listen to your teacher give the mini-lesson on the 13 moons, record the information that stands out to you. Feel free to use the topics below to organize your information.

SEASON OF SPRING
Sugar Moon
Sucker Moon
Flower Moon

SEASON OF SUMMER
Strawberry Moon
Raspberry/Blueberry Moon
Grain Moon

SEASON OF FALL
Corn Moon
Falling Leaves Moon
Freezing Moon

SEASON OF WINTER
Little Spirit Moon
Big Spirit Moon
Spirit Moon
Bear Moon

13.0 GUIDANCE AND CAREER STUDIES LESSON PLAN

Background Information for Teachers

Guidance and career education are essential factors in providing students with the information and resources to make good school, life, and career decisions. Indigenous students require comprehensive supports in these areas with regard to transition, retention, and graduation strategies/plans/programs. Although the success rates (acquisition of diplomas/degrees) of Indigenous students are increasing, there is still a gap that needs to be addressed. The following statistics from 2011 (Statistics Canada) are evidence of the need to close this gap:

- 48.4% of Indigenous peoples have a postsecondary qualification in comparison to 64.7% of non-Indigenous peoples in Canada. Here is the breakdown for First Nations, Métis, and Inuit:
  - Four in ten First Nations peoples have a postsecondary qualification.
  - Over half of Métis have a postsecondary qualification.
  - Just over 1/3 of Inuit have a postsecondary qualification.

Even with increasing postsecondary qualifications, Indigenous peoples are still amongst the poorest (socioeconomically) in the country.

Key Terms

transition: a time of change. During transitions, students may be offered strategies, programs, and personnel to help them achieve success in school, career, and life.

retention: the condition of keeping someone or something in place, and, in this context, of keeping students in school. Students may be offered strategies, programs, and personnel that encourage them to stay in school.

Spiritual

What does it mean to be successful? For most Indigenous students, success can be defined as the contributions they will be able to make to their communities. Indigenous graduates are role models and living examples of the achievement of dreams and visions. There are numerous Indigenous role models in Canada who have excelled in a variety fields. Resiliency and dedication are keys to their success.

Physical

Time: 75 minutes

Materials/Resources

- Website Research Organizer (RM 13.1)
- access to computer lab and Internet
- access to the Ontario Native Education Counselling Association (ONECA) website on school/career/life changes for students. Go to: <www.oneca.com/transitions/> or <https://indspire.ca/laureate/> or <http://nativeamericanresources.blogspot.ca/2007/08/role-models-leaders.html>.
- deck of playing cards
- pens

Considerations

- Encourage connections to the Indigenous community as an authentic way to build relationships and explore career opportunities.
- Do not avoid difficult conversations regarding perceptions about Indigenous peoples (e.g., unemployment statistics). Engage students respectfully.

Suggested Adaptations by Grade

9 – Explore the personal life-management skills that affect students' success in school. These may include time-management, reliability, maturity, organization, and others.

10 – Create a personal portfolio that documents students' abilities, skills, talents, hobbies, and dreams, and connect these to potential career opportunities with Indigenous communities or with a respectful Indigenous focus.

11 – Using the Transitions website from ONECA, construct a plan that documents postsecondary or work destinations with clear outcomes (e.g., training, salary, locations, opportunity for advancement, skills required).

12 – Understand the importance of transferable workplace skills in all areas of life and potential career opportunities. Participate in a role-play experience as a chance to explore these skills within an Indigenous setting.

Emotional

Learning Goal

To appreciate and explore Indigenous guidance and career resources.

***Important Note!* Share the spiritual insight and the key terms as a point of reference throughout this lesson for yourself and the students.**

Step by Step

Minds-On

1. Show a short video from the ONECA website that documents some of the changes that can occur when going from secondary to postsecondary school.
2. Tell students they are going to use the playing-card method to share information. Give each student a playing card. To begin, heart holders share with diamond holders. Have students find a partner and share a valuable piece of advice or an issue raised in the video.
3. Continue to use the playing-card method until each student has been able to share at least four times (e.g., by suits, by numbers).
4. Have students return to their seats, and invite five students to share their key learning(s) with the class.

During

1. Give each student a copy of Website Research Organizer (RM 13.1) and a pen. Review the organizer with students.
2. Take students to the computer lab, and have them access the ONECA Transitions website.
3. At the ONECA Transitions website, have them find the "Student Information" section, which will take them to pages designed specifically for students.
4. In the section "Web Resources for Students," they can access a category (or one assigned to them) that will take them to a page with lists of websites (with descriptions) that deal specifically with that topic (e.g., scholarships).
5. To complete the organizer, have each student select one website on this page and research it.
6. Remind students this is a timed activity. (The amount of time spent on the activity will depend on the length of class periods in your school and how much time you can spend in the computer lab.)
7. Once they have completed this task, organize the students into groups by research category (e.g., career planning, scholarships, employment services) to quickly and briefly share a description of the site they researched and the information they found at the site.
8. Back in the classroom, have students share their learning with the class.

Consolidation

Select one of the questions below to synthesize and contemporize the learning from the lesson.

- Can you identify common themes that emerged from the learning presented by your peers (shared at the end of During stage of this lesson)?
- From the information given, can you develop of set of instructions on how to make successful transitions from various stages in school and in life? How?
- What are some ways to stay in school? Describe.
- Can you describe how the activities from today did or did not help you in your personal guidance and career understanding?

Intellectual

Assessment

For – Viewing video on secondary to postsecondary transitions and sharing information between peers.
As – Completion of research organizer at website and sharing of findings.
Of – Responses to a select question that consolidates the guidance/career learning from today.

Extensions

- Take the students to the Indspire website, and view the variety of role models and career opportunities that are Indigenous based.
- Invite in an Indigenous education counsellor or the Indigenous lead from your school board to discuss careers respectful of Indigenous Nations.

Date: ____________________ Name: ___________________________________

Website Research Organizer

Website name:
Website description (one clear statement):
How does this website assist you and your peers in school/career/life decisions? (four points are required here) 1. 2. 3. 4.

14.0 SOCIAL SCIENCES AND THE HUMANITIES LESSON PLAN

Background Information for Teachers

On Turtle Island, Indigenous peoples created many innovations to survive and thrive on their lands. Some of the contributions emerging from the Nations on Turtle Island include: companion planting, irrigation systems, seed selection, apartment complexes, home insulation, lighthouses, stonemasonry, jewellery, pottery, weaving, almanacs, calendars, boxes, canoes, twist-on lids, mugs, popcorn poppers, bridges, seawalls, crampons, mukluks, parkas, snowshoes, trousers, beans, corn, pemmican, pumpkins, sweet potatoes, mouthwash, toothbrushes, beekeeping, parrot breeding, money, scales, tax systems, dyes, fishhooks, food colouring, freeze-drying, instant foods, maple syrup, maple sugar, potato chips, quinoa, Tabasco sauce, vanilla, camouflage, megaphones, bunk beds, hammocks, umbrellas, place names, sign language, geometry, anesthetics, oral contraception, skin grafts, stretchers, axes, ironwork, smelting, copper tubing, military tactics, bells, maracas, detergent, hair conditioners, insect-bite remedies, salve, census, labour laws, women's rights, dreamwork psychology, zoos, latex, paint rollers, pulleys, drill bits, saws, hockey, lacrosse, kayaks, and road systems.

Important Note! Many of these innovations were also developed independently across the world at different times.

Key Terms

authentic: genuine origin(s) that are undisputed and can be proven as legitimate

relationship: state and ways by which beings are connected. It can also refer to the levels of understanding and compassion between groups.

Spiritual

The contributions of Indigenous peoples on Turtle Island to the rest of the world are immense. Many of their innovations were patented (through law) by settler cultures, as Indigenous peoples were not legally in a position to patent any ideas at all. Indigenous peoples in Canada were not allowed legal representation until the early 1950s and were not allowed to vote until the 1960s. These historical outrages contributed to the appropriation of many Indigenous innovations.

Physical

Time: 75 minutes

Materials/Resources

- Contributions of Indigenous Peoples (RM 14.1)
- *American Indian Contributions to the World* by Keoke and Porterfield (2003), or go to: <http://en.wikipedia.org/wiki/Native_American_contributions> or <www.nrcs.usda.gov/Internet/FSE_DOCUMENTS/nrcs141p2_024206.pdf>
- computer/tablet with Internet access (optional)
- access to a large, open space
- footbags (commercially known as Hacky Sacks) in various sizes and colours
- pens

Considerations

- Establish a partnership with a local Indigenous community to access additional examples of contributions.
- Do not simplify the contributions as primitive. Provide more detail in descriptions by using the suggested resources.

Suggested Adaptations by Grade

9 – Demonstrate further understanding of Indigenous contributions in the specific areas of food and nutrition. Make connections by creating a recipe or recipes showing this influence.
10 – Investigate deeper connections to Indigenous contributions in the areas of traditional clothing and contemporary fashion design. Research the design work of local Nations.
11 – Generate an Indigenous contributions class portfolio focused on the themes of sociological characteristics of various Nations. Compare and contrast from the local to the national.
12 – Organize a class mural that documents the psychological contributions of Indigenous peoples to the world. These can range from dream analysis, to therapy, to healing, to influences on current trends.

Emotional

Learning Goal

To appreciate the diversity of Indigenous innovations and make personal connections to them.

Step by Step

Minds-On

1. Have students meet in an open area. Give each student a footbag. Model, or have a student model, how to use it. Allow students to play with the footbags, individually, in pairs, or in small groups for 10 minutes.
2. Have students sit down (wherever they are). Explain: "On the North American continent, footbags (which you may know as Hacky Sacks) were used by Arapaho women who created these items from the stomach linings of various animals. The women decorated the footbags, using dyes from various plants and berries on the land. Arapaho women held footbag tournaments. These tournaments were instrumental to developing women's dexterity and fitness."
3. Have students share with a partner how this information (has or has not) changed their perception of Indigenous peoples.

Important Note! Share the spiritual insight and the key terms as a point of reference throughout this lesson for yourself and the students.

During

1. Conduct a mini-lesson (using a method of your choice) on the contributions of Indigenous peoples. Contributions of Indigenous Peoples (RM 14.1), the Keoke text, or the suggested websites are excellent resources for this activity.
2. Give each student a copy of Contributions of Indigenous Peoples (RM 14.1). Review the tasks with the students. Guide them in the completing of the tasks.
3. When complete, have students share with a partner the innovations they listed on this organizer. Begin by having the students share with another who is holding a footbag of a similar colour or shape. Ensure students share with at least three other students.
4. Close this part of the lesson by facilitating a brief discussion on the last two questions from the reproducible (RM 14.1).

Consolidation

Select one of the questions below to synthesize and contemporize the learning from the lesson.

- Why are these contributions not more publicly known?
- What would happen if these contributions were publicly credited to the Indigenous Nations?
- How does this lesson connect to your learning in this course?
- Can you identify the contributions that most (and least) surprised you? Why (or why not) are you surprised?

Intellectual

Assessment

For – Playing with a footbag and sharing key insight on its origins.

As – Completion of contributions organizer (RM 14.1) and sharing with various peers.

Of – Responses to select questions that contemporize the learning from today.

Extensions

- Bring a guest speaker or Indigenous resource person into the classroom to conduct a session or workshop on a related topic.
- Go to an Indigenous community, event, or organization that addresses some part of related topics in this course.

Date: ________________ Name: ______________________________

Contributions of Indigenous Peoples

Contributions of Indigenous peoples (Source: Keoke & Porterfields' American Indian Contributions to the World): companion planting, irrigation systems, seed selection, apartment complexes, home insulation, lighthouses, stonemasonry, jewellery, pottery, weaving, almanacs, calendars, boxes, canoes, twist-on lids, mugs, popcorn poppers, bridges, seawalls, crampons, mukluks, parkas, snowshoes, trousers, beans, corn, pemmican, pumpkins, sweet potatoes, mouthwash, toothbrushes, beekeeping, parrot breeding, money, scales, tax systems, dyes, fishhooks, food colouring, freeze-drying, instant foods, maple syrup, maple sugar, potato chips, quinoa, Tabasco sauce, vanilla, camouflage, megaphones, bunk beds, hammocks, umbrellas, place names, sign language, geometry, anesthetics, oral contraception, skin grafts, stretchers, axes, ironwork, smelting, copper tubing, military tactics, bells, maracas, detergent, hair conditioners, insect-bite remedies, salve, census, labour laws, women's rights, dreamwork psychology, zoos, latex, paint rollers, pulleys, drill bits, saws, hockey, lacrosse, kayaks, road systems
Review the above list of Indigenous contributions. Circle seven contributions that stand out to you – ones that surprise you, ones you did not know about, or ones you are curious to learn more about. List them here in order of greatest surprise to least surprise. 1. 2. 3. 4. 5. 6. 7.

Date: ____________ Name: ____________________

Contributions of Indigenous Peoples (continued)

Which of the contributions above have direct relevance to your life today? Explain.
Why is this information important to know and share?

APPENDIX A

MAPS

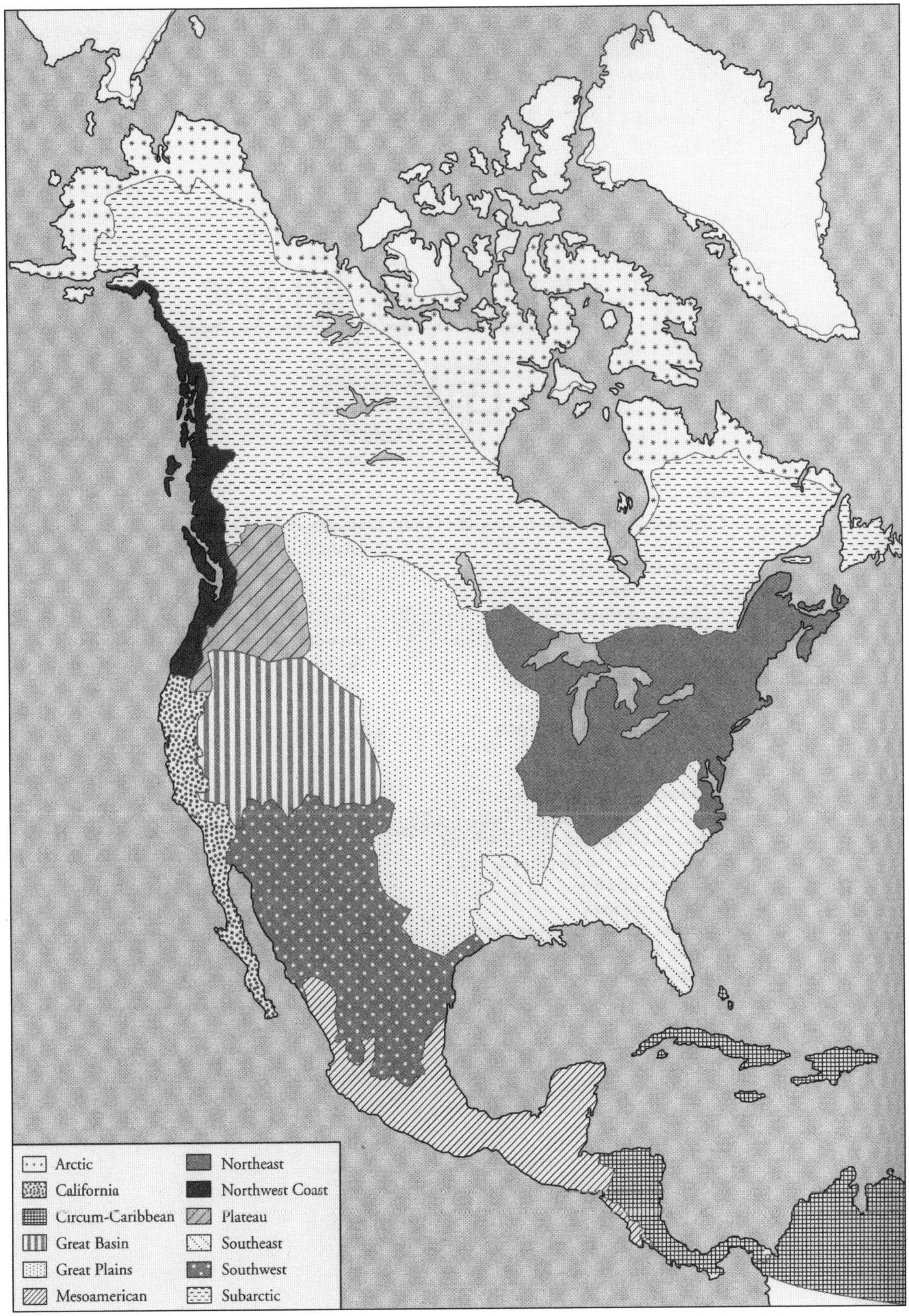

12 Geographical Regions of Turtle Island

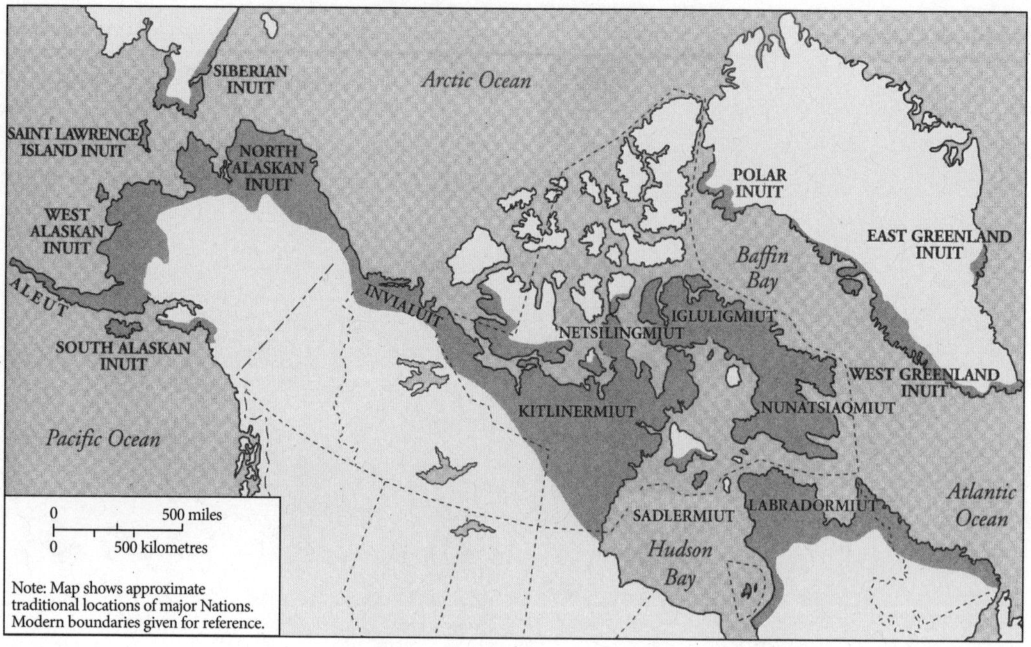

Arctic

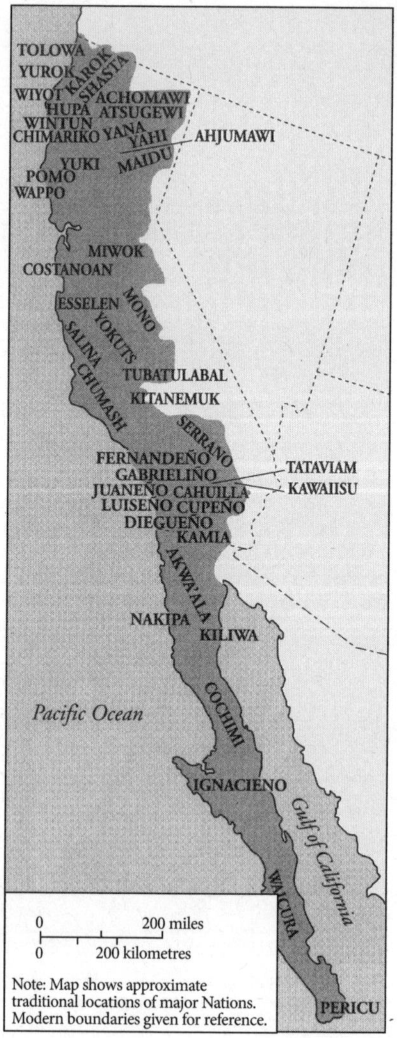

California

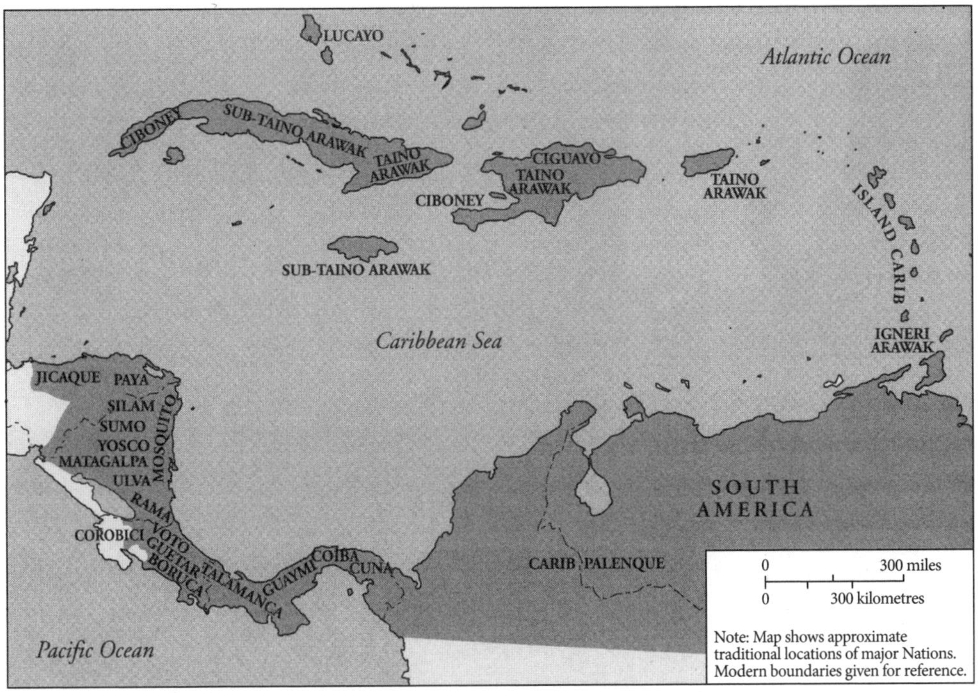

Circum-Caribbean

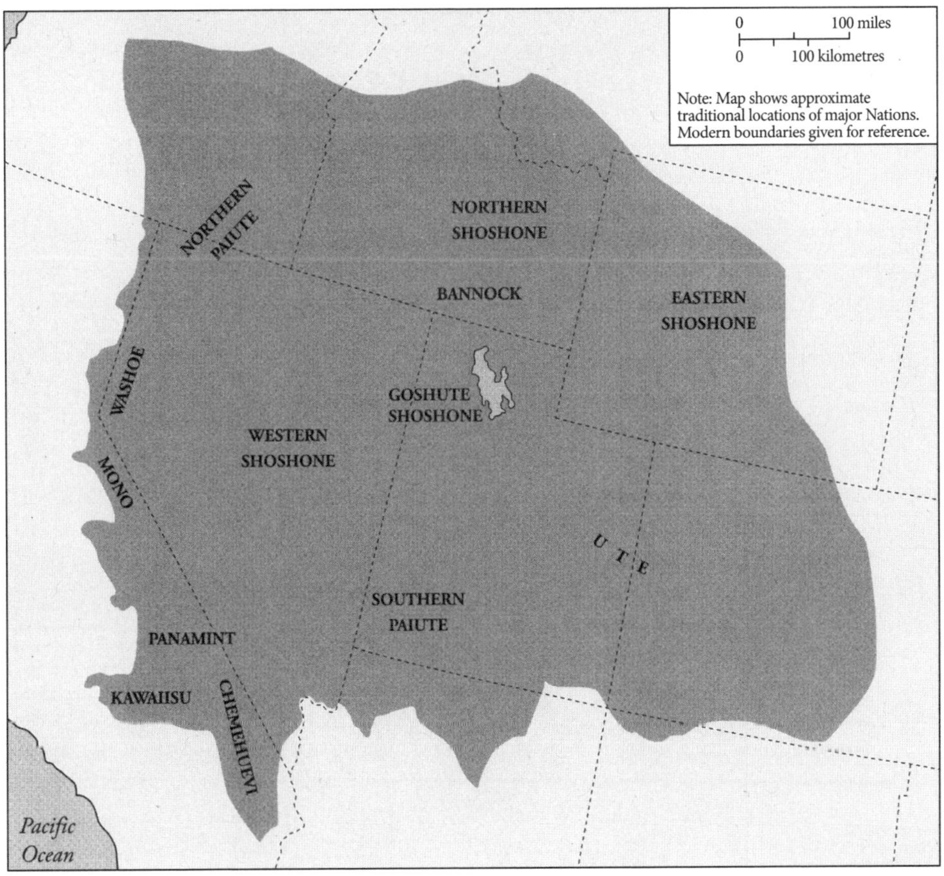

Great Basin

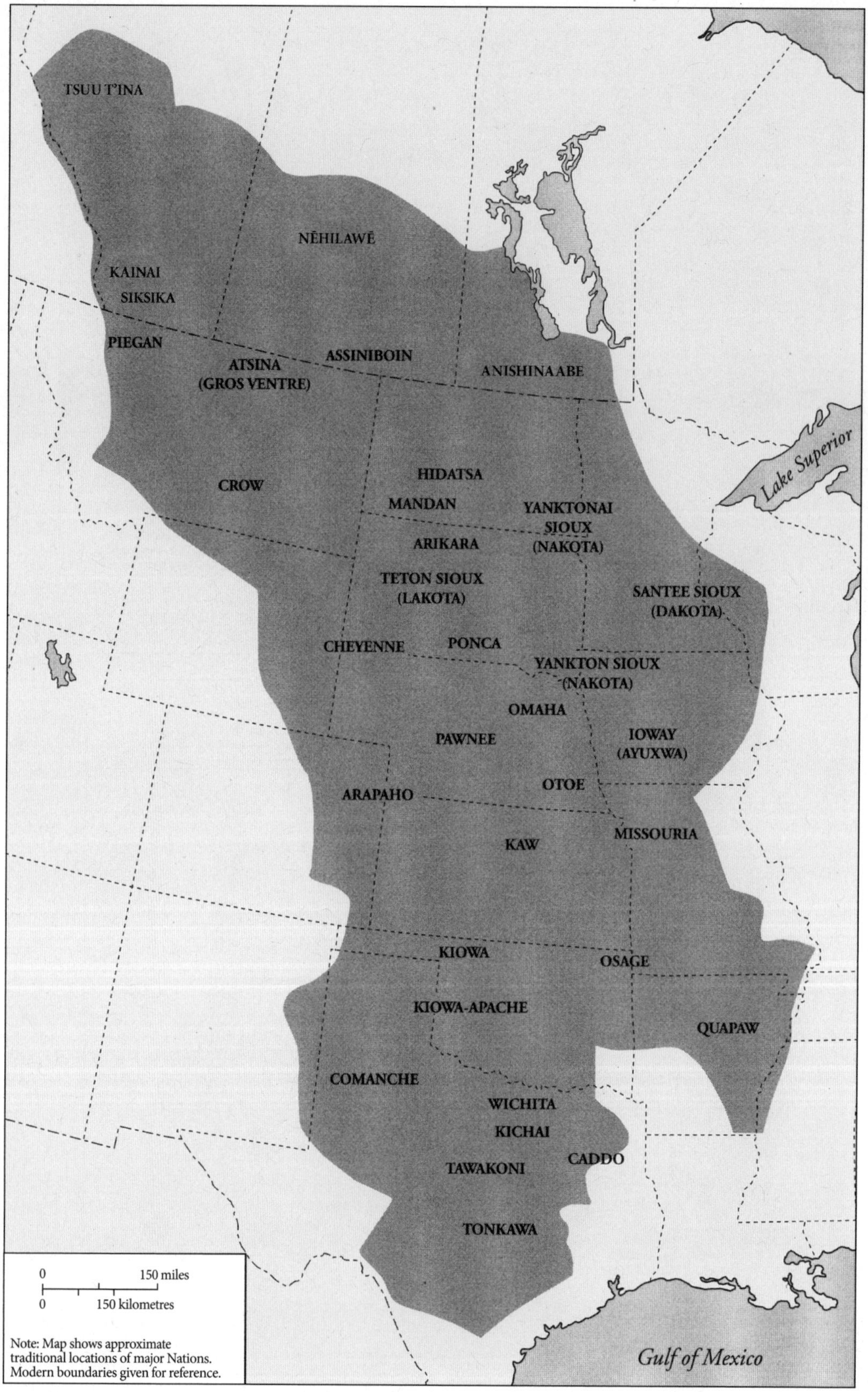

Great Plains

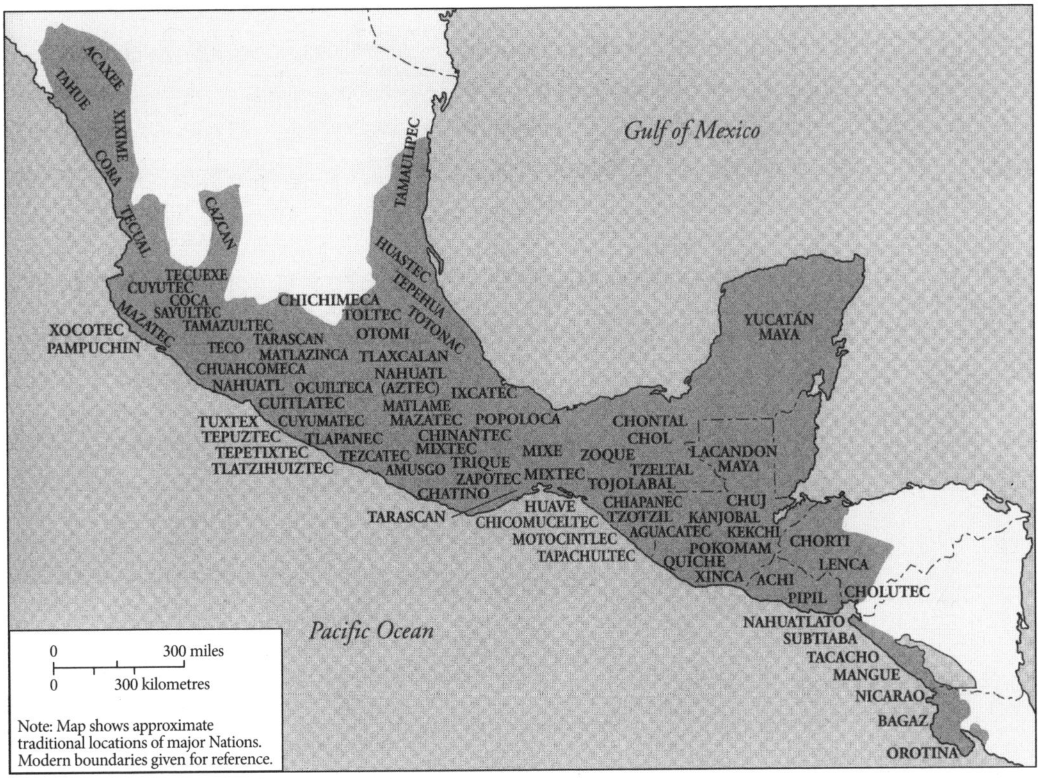

Mesoamerican

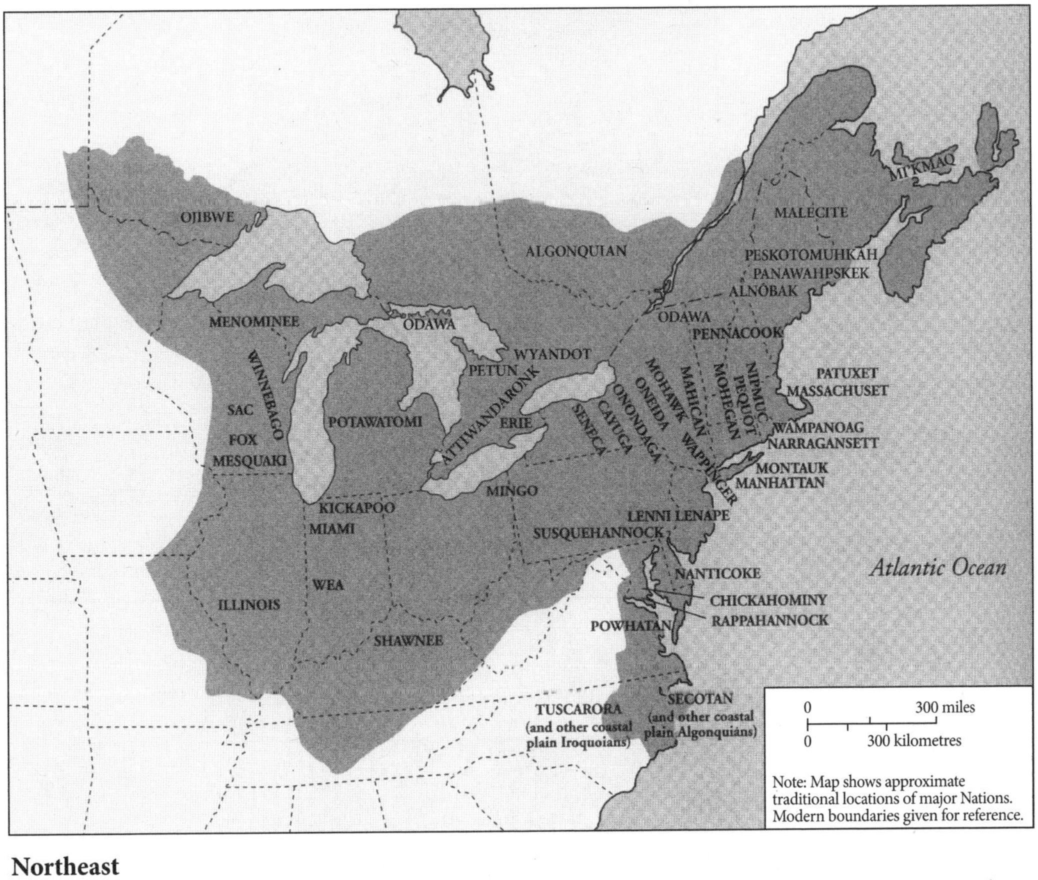

Northeast

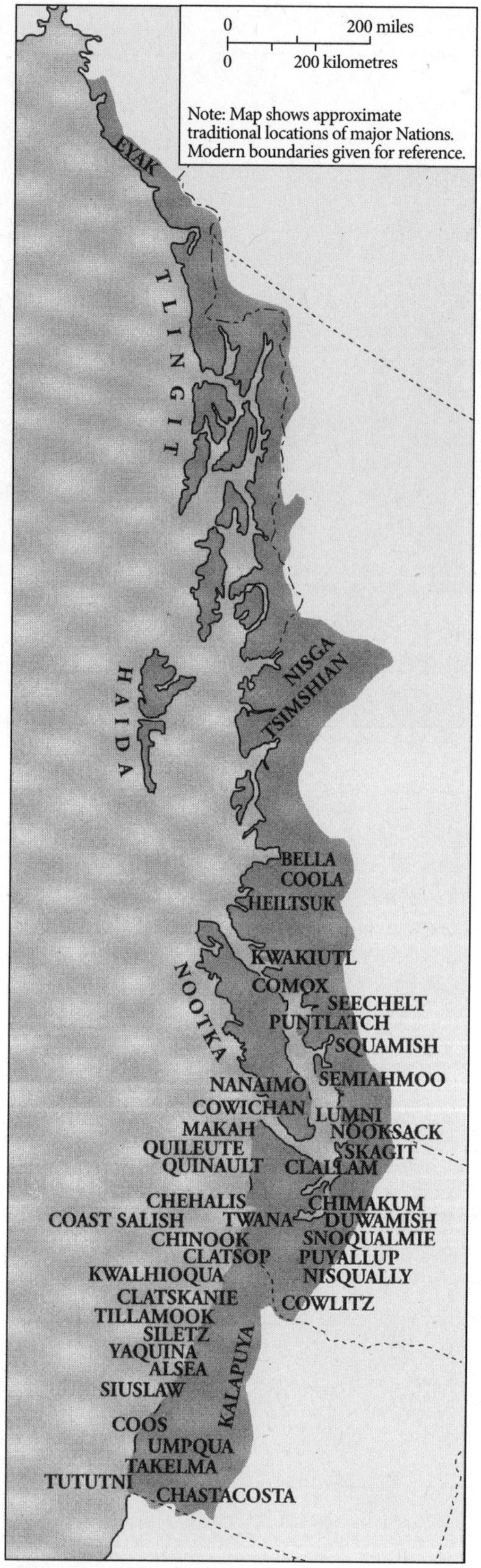

Northwest Coast

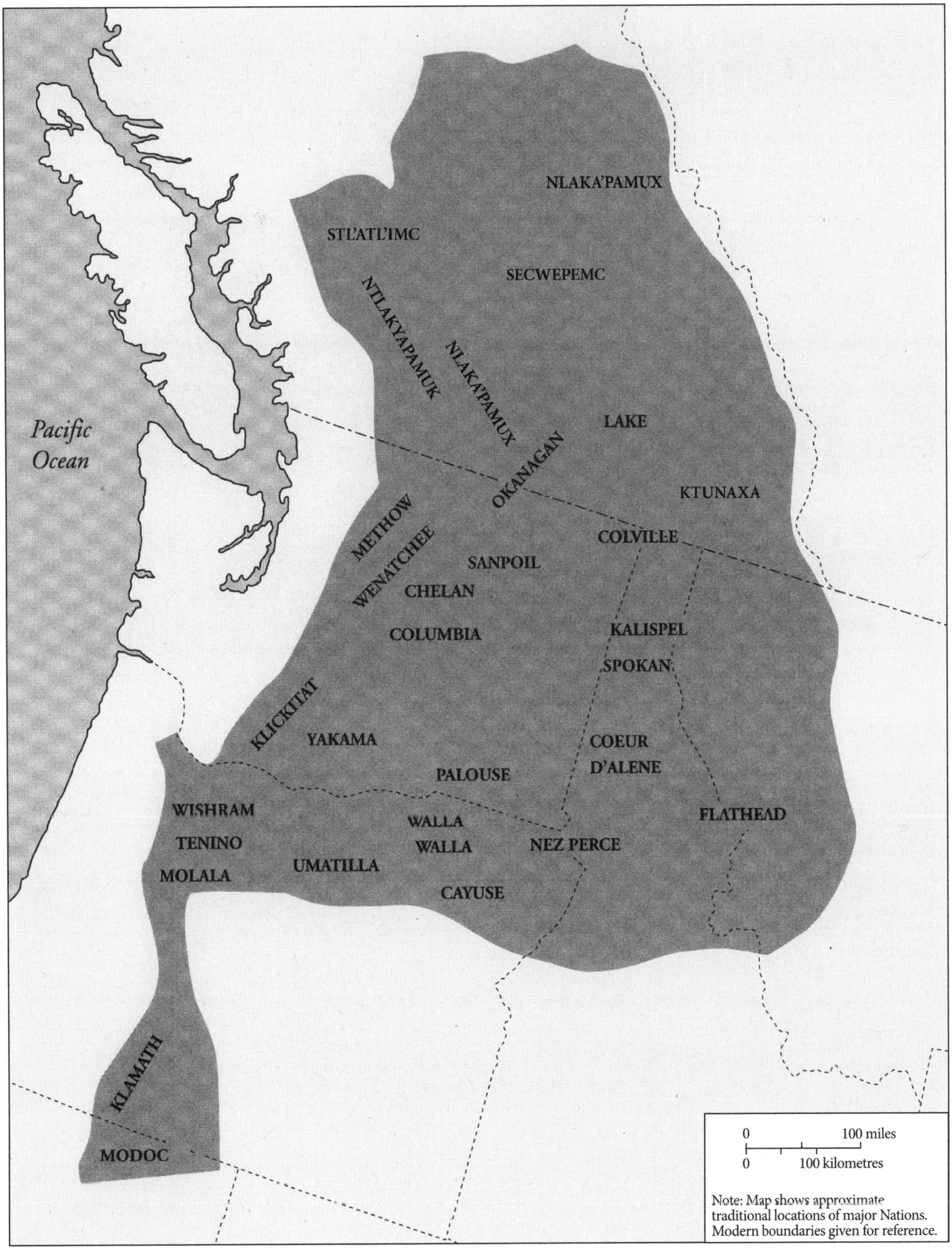
Pacific Ocean
NLAKA'PAMUX
STL'ATL'IMC
SECWEPEMC
NTLAKYAPAMUK
NLAKA'PAMUX
LAKE
OKANAGAN
KTUNAXA
METHOW
WENATCHEE
COLVILLE
SANPOIL
CHELAN
COLUMBIA
KALISPEL
SPOKAN
KLICKITAT
YAKAMA
COEUR D'ALENE
PALOUSE
WISHRAM
TENINO
MOLALA
WALLA WALLA
UMATILLA
NEZ PERCE
FLATHEAD
CAYUSE
KLAMATH
MODOC
0 100 miles
0 100 kilometres
Note: Map shows approximate traditional locations of major Nations. Modern boundaries given for reference.

Plateau

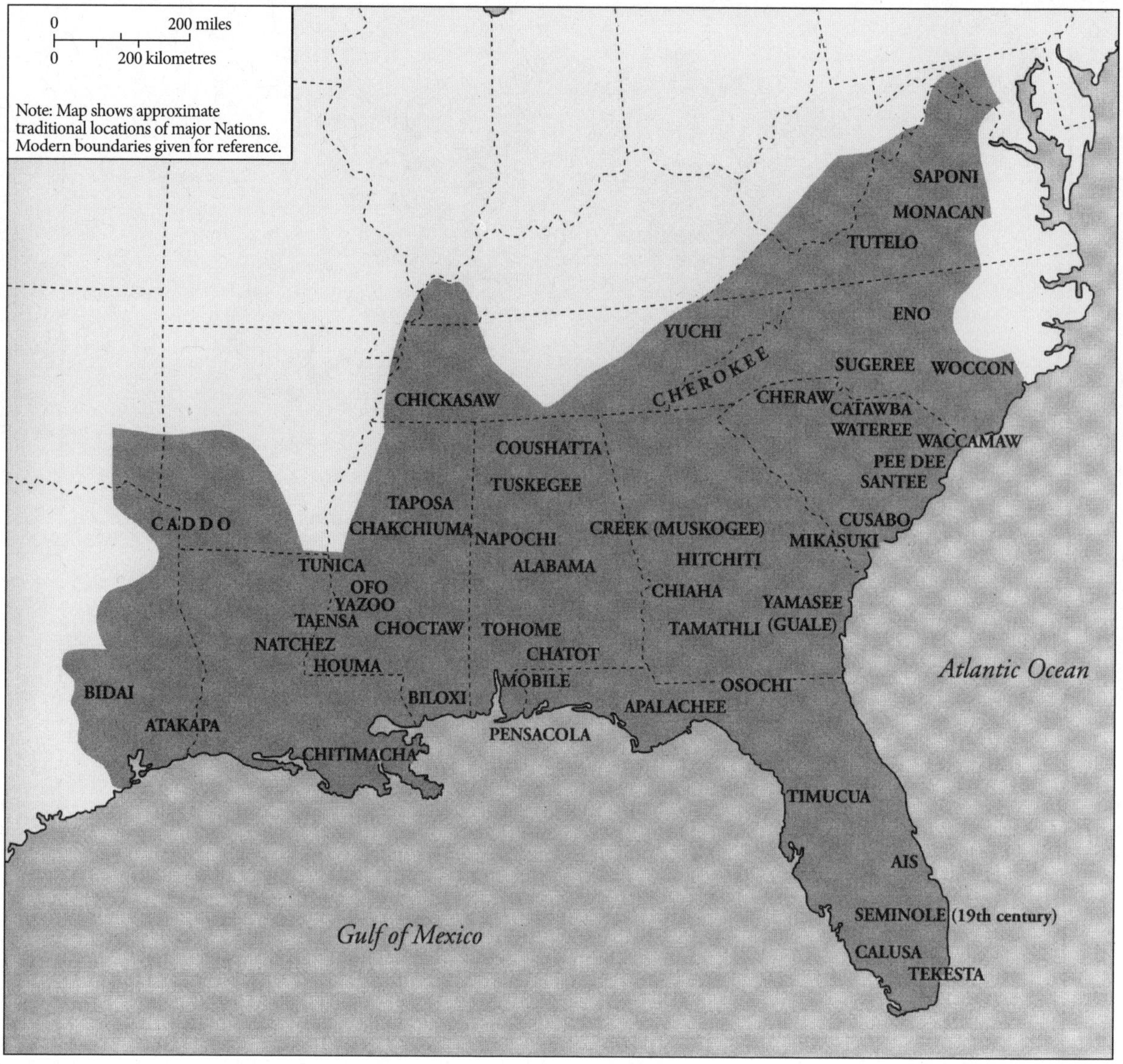
0 200 miles
0 200 kilometres
Note: Map shows approximate traditional locations of major Nations. Modern boundaries given for reference.
SAPONI
MONACAN
TUTELO
ENO
YUCHI
CHEROKEE
SUGEREE
WOCCON
CHERAW
CATAWBA
WATEREE
WACCAMAW
PEE DEE
SANTEE
CHICKASAW
COUSHATTA
TUSKEGEE
TAPOSA
CHAKCHIUMA
CADDO
NAPOCHI
CREEK (MUSKOGEE)
CUSABO
MIKASUKI
TUNICA
ALABAMA
HITCHITI
OFO
YAZOO
CHIAHA
YAMASEE
TAENSA
CHOCTAW
TOHOME
TAMATHLI
(GUALE)
NATCHEZ
HOUMA
CHATOT
Atlantic Ocean
BIDAI
MOBILE
OSOCHI
BILOXI
APALACHEE
ATAKAPA
PENSACOLA
CHITIMACHA
TIMUCUA
AIS
SEMINOLE (19th century)
Gulf of Mexico
CALUSA
TEKESTA

Southeast

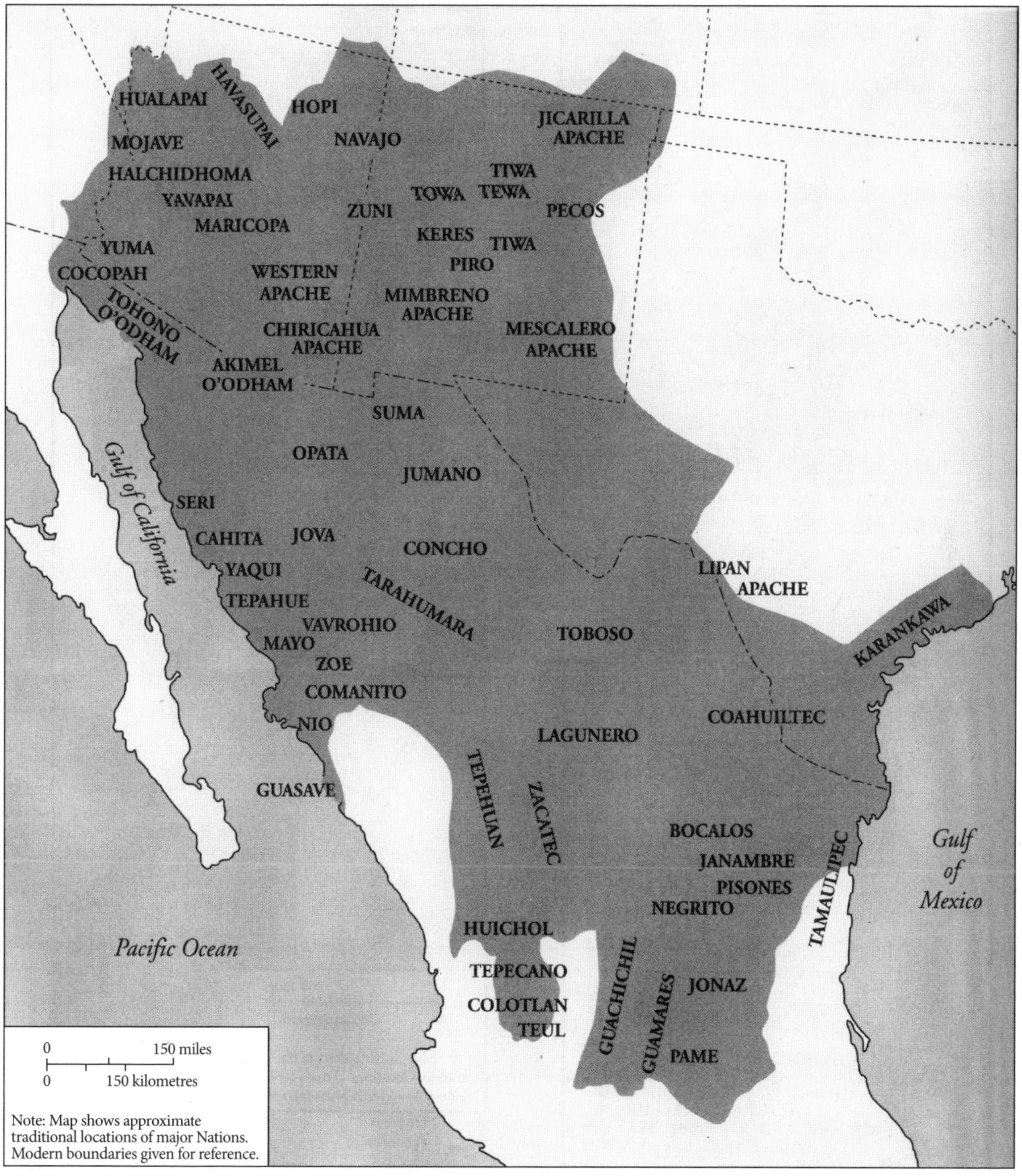
HUALAPAI
HAVASUPAI
HOPI
MOJAVE
NAVAJO
JICARILLA APACHE
HALCHIDHOMA
TIWA
TOWA
TEWA
YAVAPAI
ZUNI
PECOS
MARICOPA
KERES
TIWA
YUMA
PIRO
COCOPAH
WESTERN APACHE
MIMBRENO APACHE
TOHONO O'ODHAM
CHIRICAHUA APACHE
MESCALERO APACHE
AKIMEL O'ODHAM
SUMA
OPATA
JUMANO
Gulf of California
SERI
CAHITA
JOVA
CONCHO
YAQUI
TARAHUMARA
LIPAN APACHE
TEPAHUE
VAVROHIO
MAYO
TOBOSO
KARANKAWA
ZOE
COMANITO
COAHUILTEC
NIO
LAGUNERO
GUASAVE
TEPEHUAN
ZACATEC
BOCALOS
Gulf of Mexico
JANAMBRE
PISONES
NEGRITO
TAMAULIPEC
HUICHOL
Pacific Ocean
TEPECANO
GUACHICHIL
GUAMARES
JONAZ
COLOTLAN
TEUL
PAME
0 150 miles
0 150 kilometres
Note: Map shows approximate traditional locations of major Nations. Modern boundaries given for reference.

Southwest

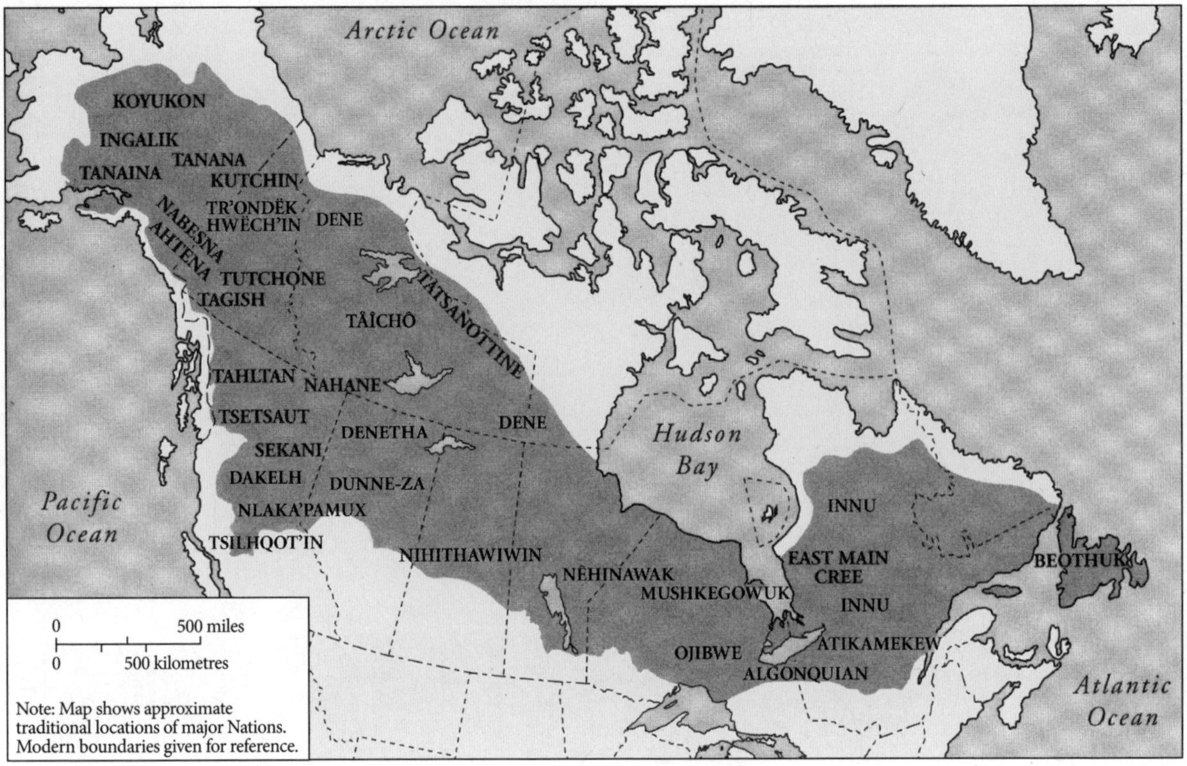
Arctic Ocean
KOYUKON
INGALIK
TANANA
TANAINA
KUTCHIN
TR'ONDËK HWËCH'IN
DENE
NABESNA
AHTENA
TUTCHONE
TAGISH
TÂÎCHÔ
TATSANOTTINE
TAHLTAN
NAHANE
TSETSAUT
DENETHA
DENE
SEKANI
DAKELH
DUNNE-ZA
NLAKA'PAMUX
TSILHQOT'IN
NIHITHAWIWIN
NÊHINAWAK
MUSHKEGOWUK
OJIBWE
ALGONQUIAN
ATIKAMEKW
EAST MAIN CREE
INNU
INNU
BEOTHUK
Hudson Bay
Pacific Ocean
Atlantic Ocean
0 500 miles
0 500 kilometres
Note: Map shows approximate traditional locations of major Nations. Modern boundaries given for reference.

Subarctic

APPENDIX B

INDIGENOUS NAMES FOR FIRST NATIONS AND INUIT OF CANADA

ALTERNATIVE NAMES FOR INDIGENOUS PEOPLES OF THE UNITED STATES

The term *The People* is a respectful way of referring to the Indigenous peoples of Canada and the United States. In traditional Indigenous languages, the names of many Nations can be translated into "The People," followed with a key descriptor (e.g., The People of the Lakes). Some names translate into "Original People" in their Native languages or make reference to the Native language originally spoken.

Indigenous Names for First Nations and Inuit of Canada

Below, beneath the geographical regions, are the anglicized names of First Nations and Inuit located in Canada. To the right are the Indigenous names.[2]

Arctic

Baffinland Inuit	Nunatsiaqmiut
Caribou Inuit	Qairnirmiut, Harvaqtuurmiut, Hauniqtuurmiut, Paallirmiut, and Ahiarmiut
Copper Inuit	Kitlinermiut
Iglulik Inuit	Igluligmiut
Labrador Inuit	Labradormiut
Mackenzie Inuit	Invialuit
Netsilik Inuit	Netsilingmiut
Southampton Inuit	Sadlermiut

Great Plains

Assiniboine	Assiniboin
Blackfoot	Siksika
Blood	Kainai
Plains Cree	Nēhilawē (also Nêhiyawak)
Plains Ojibway	Anishinaabe
Sarcee	Tsuu T'ina

Northeast

Abenaki	Alnôbak
Algonkin	Algonquian
Chippewa	Ojibwe
Erie	Erie
Huron	Wyandot
Iroquois	Haudensonee
Maliseet	Malecite
Micmac	Mi'kmaq
Neutral	Attiwandaronk or
Chonnonton	
Ottawa	Odawa
Passamaquody	Peskotomuhkah
Penobscot	Panawahpskek
Tobacco	Petun

Northwest Coast

Bella Coola	Nuxalk/Oweekeno
Comox	K'ómoks
Cowichan	Cowichan
Haida	Haida
Heiltsuk	Heiltsuk
Kwakiutl	Kwakwa̲ka̲/Oweekeno
Nanaimo	Snuneymuxw
Niisga	Nisga'a
Nootka	Nuu-chah-nulth
Seechelt	Shishálh
Semiahmoo	Semiahmoo
Squamish	Sk̲wx̱wú7mesh
Tlingit	Tlingit
Tsimshian	Gitx̱san

Plateau

Kootenai	Ktunaxa
Lillooet	Stl'atl'imc
Nicola	Nlaka'pamux
Ntlakyapamuk	Ntlakyapamuk
Okanagan	Okanagan
Shuswap	Secwepemc
Thompson	Nlaka'pamux

Subarctic

Algonkin	Algonquian
Beaver	Dunne-za
Beothuk	Beothuk
Carrier	Dakelh/Wet'suwet'en
Chilcotin	Tsilhqot'in
Chipewyan	Dene
Chippewa	Ojibwe
Dogrib	Tåîchô
East Main Cree	
Han	Tr'ondëk Hwëch'in
Hare	Dene
Kutchin	Gwich'in

2 The spellings of many Indigenous-named First Nations and Inuit of Canada vary, depending on the source. Names that could not be located have been left blank.

Subarctic

Montagnais	Innu
Naskapi	Innu
Sekani	Sekani
Slave	Dene Tha
Swampy Cree	Nêhinawak
Tagish	Taglish
Tahltan	Tahltan
Tatsanottine	Tatsanottine
Tête de Boule Cree	Atikamekew
Thompson	Nlaka'pamux
Tsetsaut	Tsetsaust
Tutchone	Tutchone
West Main Cree	Mushkegowuk
Western Woods Cree	Nihithawiwin

Alternative Names for Indigenous Peoples of the United States

The names of the American Indigenous Nations that appear on the maps in appendix A are listed below, beneath the geographical regions. Many Indigenous Nations in the United States still go by these names. Many other Nations, however, use alternatives names of self-identification. While the list below is incomplete, some of these alternative names can be found to the right of the more common names.[3]

Arctic

Aleut	Unangan
North Alaskan Inuit	
Saint Lawrence Island Inuit	
South Alaskan Inuit	
West Alaskan Inuit	

California

Achomawi	
Ahjumawi	
Akwa'ala	
Atsugewi	
Cahuilla	ʔiviĬuqaletem
Chimariko	
Chumash	sʔamala /sʔamala
Cochmi	
Costanoan	Ohlone
Cupeno	Kuupangaxwichem
Diegueno	Kumeyaay
Esselen	
Fernandeno	Tataviam
Gabrielino	Tongva
Hupa	Natinook-wa
Ignacieno	
Juaneno	Acjachemen
Kamia	Kumeyaay
Karok	
Kawaiisu	Nuwa
Kiliwa	K'olew
Kitanemuk	
Luiseno	Payómkawichum
Maidu	
Miwok	
Mono	Nyyhmy
Nakipa	
Pericu	
Pomo	
Salina	
Serrano	Taaqtam
Shasta	
Tataviam	Tongva
Tolowa	Taa-laa-wa Dee-ni
Tubatulabal	Tübatulabal
Waicura	Guaycura
Wappo	
Wintun	
Wiyot	
Yahi	
Yana	
Yokuts	
Yuki	
Yurok	Olekwo

Great Basin

Bannock	Banakwat
Chemehuevi	Nüwüwü
Eastern Shoshone	
Goshute Shoshone	Kutsipiuti
Kawaiisu	Nuwa
Mono	Nyyhmy
Northern Paiute	Numa
Northern Shoshone	Nimi
Panamint	Timbisha Shoshone

3 The spellings of many Indigenous names vary, depending on the source.

Great Basin

Southern Paiute	Nuwunvi
Ute	Nunt'zi
Washoe	
Western Shoshone	Newe

Great Plains

Arapaho	Hinonoeino
Arikara	Sahnish
Atsina (Gros Ventre)	A'aninin
Caddo	Kadohadacho/Hasinai
Cheyenne	Tsétsêhéstâhese /Só'taeo'o
Comanche	Nʉmʉnʉʉ
Crow	Apssálooke
Hidatsa	Hiraacá
Ioway (Ayuxwa)	Baxoje/Pahoja
Kaw	Kanza
Kichai	K'itaish
Kiowa	
Kiowa	Ka'igwa
Kiowa-Apache	
Mandan	Nueta
Missouria	Nutachi
Omaha	Umonhon
Osage	Niukonska
Otoe	Jiwere
Pawnee	Chahiksichahiks
Piegan	Pikuni
Ponca	Panka
Quapaw	Ugakhpa
Santee Sioux	Dakota
Sioux	Nakota
Tawakoni	
Teton Sioux	Lakota
Tonkawa	Titska Watich
Wichita	Kitikiti'sh
Yankton Sioux	Nakota
Yanktonai	Iháŋkthuŋwaŋna

Northeast

Abenaki	Alnombak
Cayuga	Gayogohó:no'
Chickahominy	
Fox	Meakwahkihaki
Illinois	Illiniwek
Kickapoo	Kiwigapawa
Lenni Lenape	
Manhattan	
Massachuset	
Menominee	Mamaceqtaw
Mesquaki	Meakwahkihaki
Miami	Twightwee
Mingo	Mingwe
Mohawk	Kanienkehaka
Mohegan	Mohingen
Montauk	
Nanticoke	Nantego
Narragansett	Nanigansek
Nipmuc	8miskan8ak8iak
Oneida	Onyoda'aka
Onondaga	Onundaga'ono
Patuxet	
Pennacook	Penakuk
Pequot	
Potawatomi	Bode'wadmi
Powhatan	
Rappahannock	
Sac	Sa ki wa ki
Secotan	
Seneca	Onodawaga
Shawnee	Shawanwa
Susquehanncock	Andaste
Tuscarora	Skarooren
Wampanoag	
Wappinger	
Wea	waayaahtanwa
Winnebago	Ho-Chunk

Northwest Coast

Alsea	
Chastacosta	Shista Kwŭsta
Chehalis	
Chimakum	
Chinook	
Clallam	nəxʷsƛay'əm
Clatskanie	
Clatsop	
Coast Salish	
Coos	
Cowlitz	
Dumakum	
Kalapuya	
Kwalhioqua	
Lumni	Lhaq'temish
Makah	
Nisqually	
Nooksack	Noxws'áʔaq
Puyallup	S'Puyalupubsh
Quileute	Quillayute
Quinault	
Siletz	

Northwest Coast

Siuslaw	
Skagit	
Snoqualmie	Sduqwalbixw
Takelma	
Tillamook	
Tututni	
Twana	Skokmish
Umpqua	
Yaquina	

Plateau

Cayuse	Tetawken
Chelan	Tsi-Laan
Columbia	Sinkiuse-Columbia
Colville	Shuyelpee
Couer D'alene	Schitsu'umsh
Flathead	Salish
Kalispel	Qlispé
Klamath	Maklak
Klickitat	Qwulhhwaipum
Methow	
Modoc	Maklak
Molala	
Nez Perce	Niimiipo
Okanagan	Syilx
Palouse	
Sanpoil	Nesīlextel'n
Spokan	Sqeliz
Tenino	
Umatilla	
Walla Walla	
Wenatchee	
Wishram	Tlakluit/Echeloot
Yakama	Mamachatpam

Southeast

Ais	
Alabama	
Apalachee	
Atakapa	Yuk'hitlishak
Bidai	
Biloxi	Tanaka-haya
Caddo	Kadawdaachuh
Calusa	
Catawba Wateree	Iswa
Chatot	
Cheraw	
Cherokee	Ani'yunwi'ya
Chiana	
Chickasaw	Chickasha

Southeast

Chitimacha	
Choctaw	Chahta
Coushatta	Koasati
Creek (Muskogee)	
Cusabo	
Eno	Wyanoak
Hitchiti	
Houma	
Mikasuki	Miccosukee
Mobile	
Monacan	
Napochi	
Natchez	
Ofo	
Osochi	
Pee Dee Santee	
Pensacola	
Saponi	
Seminole	Yat'siminole
Sugeree	
Taensa	
Tamathli	
Taposa	
Tekesta	
Timucua	Thimogna
Tohome	
Tunica	Yoron
Tuskegee	
Tutelo	Yesan
Waccamaw	
Woccon	
Yamasee (Guale)	
Yazoo	
Yuchi	Tsoyaha

Southwest

Akimel O'Odham	
Apache	
Bolcalos	
Cahita	
Chiricahua Apache	
Coahuiltec	
Cocopah	Xawitt kwñchawaay
Colotlan	
Comanito	
Concho	Tapaxcolmch
Guachichil	Quauhchichití
Guamares	
Guasave	
Halchidhoma	Xalychidom Piipaa

Southwest

Havasupai	
Hopi	
Hualapai	
Huichol	Wíxáritarí
Janambre	
Jicarilla Apache	Tinde
Jonaz	
Jova	
Jumano	Xumani
Karankawa	Auía
Keres	
Lagunero	
Lipan	Lépai-Ndé
Maricopa	Piipaa
Mayo	Yoreme
Mescalero Apache	Shis-Inday
Mimbreno Apache	
Mojave	
Navajo	Diné
Negrito	
Opata	
Pame	
Pecos	
Piro	
Pisones	
Seri	Comcaac
Suma	

Southwest

Tamaulipec	
Tarahumara	
Tepahue	Tepehuanes
Tepecano	
Tepehuan	Tepehuanes
Tewa	
Tiwa	
Toboso	
Tohono O'Odham	
Towa	
Tuec	
Vavrohio	
Western Apache	Ndeh
Yaqui	Haiki
Yavapai	
Yuma	
Zacatec	Nahuatl Zacatecatl
Zoe	Zo'é
Zuni	A:shiwi

Subarctic

Ahtena	
Ingalik	Deg Hit'an
Koyukon	
Nabesna	
Tanana	
Tanaina	Dena'ina

REFERENCES

Aboriginal Literacy Foundation. 2012. *Aboriginal education: New pathways in learning and teaching,* ed. Anthony Cree. Auckland, NZ: Australasian Combined Universities Press.

Alberta Education. 2011. *Curriculum handbook for parents (multiple grades).* Edmonton, AB: Government of Alberta.

Anuik, J. D. 2014. Indian control of Indian education at 40: Assessment of First Nations education policy in the post-control era. *Alberta Journal of Educational Research* 59.3: 529–34.

Assembly of First Nations. 2012a. *First Nations lifelong learning assessment report.* Ottawa, ON: AFN.

______. 2012b. *Supporting First Nations learners transitioning to post-secondary.* Ottawa, ON: AFN.

Association of Universities and Colleges of Canada (Universities Canada). 2013. *Creating opportunities in education for Aboriginal students.* Ottawa, ON: AUCC.

Barman, J. 2011. Schooled for inequality: The education of British Columbia Aboriginal children. In *Schooling in transition: Readings in Canadian history of education,* ed. Sara Z. Burke and Patrice Milewski, 255. Toronto: University of Toronto Press.

Battiste. M. 2013. *Decolonizing education: Nourishing the learning spirit.* Saskatoon, SK: Purich Publishing.

______. 2011. Enabling the autumn seed: Toward a decolonized approach to Aboriginal knowledge, language, and education. In *Schooling in transition: Readings in Canadian history of education,* ed. Sara Z. Burke and Patrice Milewski, 275–86. Toronto: University of Toronto Press.

Baxter, D. 2006. *Aboriginal presence in our schools: A guide for staff.* Thunder Bay, ON: Lakehead Public Schools.

Bell, D., et al. 2004. *Sharing our success: Ten case studies in Aboriginal schooling.* Kelowna, BC: Society for the Advancement of Excellence in Education.

best start/meilleur depart. 2011. *A child becomes strong: Journeying through each stage of the life cycle.* Toronto: health nexus sante.

Brooks, Cassandra. 2009. *Two worlds working together: Forming a link between traditional knowledge and western science.* sacnas.org/about/stories/sacnas-news/fall-2009/two-worlds-working-together (accessed August 17, 2009).

Burack, J. A., et al. 2014. Developmental perspectives on the role of cultural identity in well-being: Evidence from Aboriginal communities in Canada. In *Cultural and contextual perspectives on developmental risk and well-being,* ed. J.A. Burack and L.A. Schmidt. New York: Cambridge University Press.

Canadian Council on Learning. 2007. *Redefining how success is measured in First Nations, Inuit and Métis learning: Report in learning in Canada.* Ottawa, ON: CCL.

Canadian Encyclopedia. 2013. *Aboriginal art in Canada.* www.thecanadianencyclopedia.ca/en/article/aboriginal-art-in-canada/.

Chiefs Assembly on Education. 2012. *A portrait of First Nations and education.* Gatineau, QC: Palais des Congres de Gatineau.

Council of Ministers of Education, Canada. 2010. *A literature review of factors that support successful transitions by Aboriginal people from K–12 to postsecondary education.* Toronto: Statistics Canada.

Darshana, A. 2014. *Bloom objectives planning worksheet 2.* www.docstoc.com/docs/164472053/Bloom-objectives-planning-worksheet-2aqvoxu (accessed March 14, 2014).

Deer, F. 2013a. Integrating Aboriginal perspectives in education: Perceptions of pre-service teachers. *Canadian Journal of Education/Revue canadienne de l'éducation* 36.2: 175–211.

______. 2013b. Aboriginal identity: A perspective on hegemony and the implications for Canadian citizenship. *in education* 17.3.

Dion, S. D., K. Johnston, and C. M. Rice. 2010. *Decolonizing our schools: Aboriginal education in the Toronto district school board.* Toronto: York University.

Donovan, S. 2011. Challenges to and successes in urban Aboriginal education in Canada: A case study of Wiingashki secondary school. In *Aboriginal peoples in Canadian cities: Transformations and continuities,* ed. H.A. Howard and C. Proulx, 123. Waterloo, ON: Wilfrid Laurier University Press.

Friesen, J., and B. Krauth. 2012. *Key policy issues in Aboriginal education: An evidence-based approach.* Toronto: Council of Ministers of Education, Canada.

Friesen, J. B., and A. N. Ezeife. 2013. Making science assessment culturally valid for Aboriginal students. In *Approaches to Aboriginal education in Canada: Searching for solutions,* ed. F. Widdowson and A. Howard, 64. Edmonton, AB: Brush Education.

Gollan, S., and M. Malin. 2012. Teachers and families working together to build stronger futures for our children in schools. In *Reform and resistance in Aboriginal education,* ed. Q. Beresford, G. Partington, and G. Gower, 149–73. Perth, WA: University of Western Australia.

Goulet, L., and Y. McLeod. 2013. Connections and reconnections: Affirming cultural identity in Aboriginal teacher education. In *Approaches to Aboriginal education in Canada: Searching for solutions,* ed. F. Widdowson and A. Howard, 100. Brush Education, Edmonton.

Government of Ontario. 2013. *Supporting minds: An educator's guide to student mental health.* Toronto: Queen's Printer for Ontario.

Gray, J., and G. Partington. 2012. Attendance and non-attendance at school. In *Reform and resistance in Aboriginal education,* ed. Q. Beresford, G. Partington, and G. Gower, 261–303. Perth, WA: University of Western Australia.

Greer, J., et al. 2011. Responding to the call for action on Aboriginal education: The role of centres for teaching and learning. http://dalspace.library.dal.ca/handle/10222/52628?show=full

Gregory, G. H., and L. E. Herndon. 2010. *Differentiated instructional strategies for the block schedule.* Thousand Oaks, CA: Corwin.

Hardes, J. 2013. Retention of Aboriginal students in post-secondary education. In *Approaches to Aboriginal education in Canada: Searching for solutions,* ed. F. Widdowson and A. Howard, 247. Edmonton, AB: Brush Education.

Huber, T. 2010. *Storied inquiries in international landscapes: An anthology of educational research.* Charlotte, NC: Information Age Publishing.

Johnson, T. L. 2013. *Instructional strategies: Supporting differentiation in the secondary classroom.* www.stcloudstate.edu/tpi/teachersupport/documents/ (accessed December 5, 2013).

Kanu, Y. 2011. *Integrating Aboriginal perspectives into the school curriculum: Purposes, possibilities, and challenges.* Toronto: University of Toronto Press.

Keoke, E. D., and K. M. Porterfield. 2003. *Encyclopedia of American Indian contributions to the world: 15 000 years of inventions and innovations.* New York: Facts On File.

Kumar, M. P. 2011. Aboriginal education in Canada: A postcolonial analysis. *AlterNative: An International Journal of Indigenous Peoples* 5.1.

Lamb, D. 2014. Aboriginal early school leavers on- and off-reserve: An empirical analysis. *Canadian Public Policy* 1–10.

Lowan, G. 2010. Exploring place from an Aboriginal perspective: Considerations for outdoor and environmental education. *Canadian Journal of Environmental Education* (CJEE) 14: 42–58.

Marzano, R. J., and J. S. Kendall. 2007. *The new taxonomy of educational objectives (2nd edition).* Thousand Oaks, CA: Corwin.

Mikkonen, J., and D. Raphael. 2010. *Social determinants of health: The Canadian facts.* Toronto: York University School of Health Policy and Management.

Munzenmaier, C., and N. Rubin. 2013. *Perspectives – Bloom's taxonomy: What's old is new again.* Santa Rosa, CA: The ELearning Guild Research.

Nardozi, A., et al. 2014. Deepening knowledge to inspire action: Including Aboriginal perspectives in teaching practice. *in education* 19.3.

Nicol, C., and L. Korteweg. 2010. Braiding teacher lives into relation: The steps and dilemmas of culturally responsive teacher education in Canada. In *Proceedings of the Eighth International Conference on Self-Study of Teacher Education Practices,* ed. L. Erickson, J. Young, and S. Pinnegar, 183–87. Herstmonceux Castle, East Sussex England; Provo, Utah: Brigham Young University.

Northey, S. S. 2005. *Handbook on differentiated instruction for middle and high schools.* New York: Eye on Education.

Ontario Ministry of Education. 2010. *Student success: Differentiated instruction educator's package.* Toronto: Queen's Printer for Ontario.

Ontario Ministry of Education. 2002. *Teaching/learning companion.* Toronto: Queen's Printer for Ontario.

Rainbow District School Board. 2013. *First Nation, Métis and Inuit presence in Rainbow schools.* Sudbury, ON: Rainbow District School Board.

Richards, J. 2013. Assessing the role of provincial education systems and reserve "non-systems." In *Interprovincial variation in Aboriginal student performance.* Conference draft (21 April 2013).

Santoro, N., et al. 2011. Teaching Indigenous children: Listening to and learning from Indigenous teachers. *Australian Journal of Teacher Education* 36.10: 5.

Scully, A. 2012. Decolonization, reinhabitation and reconciliation: Aboriginal and place-based education. *Canadian Journal of Environmental Education* (CJEE) 17: 148–58.

Statistics Canada. 2014. *Aboriginal peoples in Canada: First Nations people, Métis and Inuit.* Ottawa, ON: Statistics Canada.

St. Denis, V. 2011. Silencing Aboriginal curricular content and perspectives through multiculturalism: There are other children here. *Review of Education, Pedagogy, and Cultural Studies* 33.4: 306–17.

Steinhardt School of Culture, Education, and Human Development. 2008. *Culturally responsive differentiated instructional strategies.* New York: Metropolitan Center for Urban Education.

teachthought. *14 brilliant Bloom's taxonomy posters for teachers.* www.teachthought.com/critical-thinking/blooms-taxonomy/14-brilliant-blooms-taxonomy-posters-for-teachers/ (accessed February 2, 2014).

Toulouse, P. 2014. Bringing First Nations, Métis and Inuit contributions to the world into the K–12 curriculum. *Education Canada* 54.3: 20–24.

Toulouse, P. 2013. *Fostering literacy success for First Nations, Métis and Inuit students. What works? Research into practice.* Toronto: The Literacy and Numeracy Secretariat.

Toulouse, P. 2010. *Walk in our moccasins: A comprehensive study of Aboriginal education counsellors in Ontario.* Atikameksheng, ON: Ontario Native Education Counselling Association.

Toulouse, P. 2007. *Aboriginal student self-esteem: A living teachings approach.* Toronto: Ministry of Education Research Symposium Series.

Usalcas, J. 2010. Aboriginal people and the labour market: Estimates from the labour force survey, 2008–2010. Ottawa, ON: Statistics Canada.

Whitley, J. 2014. Supporting educational success for Aboriginal students: Identifying key influences. *McGill Journal of Education/Revue des sciences de l'éducation de McGill* 49.1: 155–81.

Widdowson, F., and A. Howard, eds. 2013. *Approaches to Aboriginal education in Canada: Searching for solutions.* Edmonton, AB: Brush Education.

Youth Development Committee. 2012. *Stepping stones: A resource on youth development.* Toronto: Government of Ontario.

IMAGE CREDITS

pages 74–75: Drawings by Jess Dixon

page 80: Minnesota Historical Society. Made by (possibly): Smith, Sophia

page 84 (top): Courtesy of Manitobah Mukluks Storyboot Artist – Meagan Anishinabie, Oji-Cree Artisan from Sandy Lake First Nation, Ontario

page 84 (middle): Courtesy of Manitobah Mukluks Storyboot Artist – Roberta Anderson, Cree Artisan from George Gordon First Nation, Saskatchewan

page 84 (bottom): Courtesy of Manitobah Mukluks Storyboot Artist – Rosa Scribe, Cree Artisan of Norway house, Manitoba

page 104: Drawings by Jess Dixon

page 119: Courtesy of Brenda Stevens, originally of the Saugeen First Nation but now of the Shawanaga First Nation, Ontario. Photos taken and submitted by the Wolf Den, Parry Sound, Ontario

page 120: Courtesy UBC Museum of Anthropology, Vancouver, Canada. Object ID #A7065 Kyla Bailey

page 124: Minnesota Historical Society. Photographer: Wright, Kenneth Melvin

page 138: Drawing by Jess Dixon

MAP CREDITS

page 95: Doug Fast

pages 101, 153–162: Adapted from *Encyclopedia of American Indian Contributions to the World: 15 000 Years of Inventions and Innovations*, by E. D. Keoke and K. M. Porterfield. New York: Facts on File, 2003